'I fully endorse the underlying assumption of t
ment of development (wellbeing) must be *multidimensional and allot
equal value to non-economic and economic aspects of "progress".*
The authors posit a fresh critical thesis by arguing that *education is
a necessary but insufficient indicator of wellbeing, in the absence of
empowerment'*.

Anne Benjamin, Honorary Professor of Australian Catholic University,
Honorary Fellow of the University of Western Sydney, Fellow of the
Australian College of Educators and Fellow of the Australian Council
of Educational Leaders.

Empowering Marginalised Women in Remote Indian Villages

Saikia, Chalmers, Michael and Orrell explore the impact of social education on gender inequalities in rural Tamil Nadu where highland women's lives are damaged by discrimination, marginalisation and deprivation. Social education refers to agent-oriented learning experiences focused on power relations designed to help oppressed people regain their humanity in the struggle for empowerment.

The book begins with the recognition that wellbeing is dependent on access to opportunities given that gender parity in tertiary education has not transferred to good jobs. This implies education is a necessary but insufficient indicator of wellbeing in the absence of empowerment. Hence, it investigates interconnections between empowerment (self-efficacy, social action and human rights) and multiple dimensions of wellbeing (living standards/livelihoods, physical and mental health, and education). It articulates how such hopes and expectations are empirically founded, thereby presenting some of the answers that readers need to move from grievance to a future that is more conducive to friendships and mutuality.

A vital resource for scholars, students, researchers and professionals interested in development studies, human rights (law and social science), anthropology of development, gender in development, public health administration, governance/public administration, and welfare economics.

Udoy Saikia is a Professor at the College of Humanities, Arts and Social Sciences in Flinders University, Adelaide, South Australia.

Jim Chalmers is an Associate Professor (Adjunct) at the College of Humanities, Arts and Social Sciences in Flinders University, Adelaide, South Australia.

Dency Michael is the Executive Director of the Kodaikanal Grihini Trust and former Director of the Grihini Programme.

Janice Orrell is a Professor Emeritus of Flinders University and Adjunct Full Professor of Higher Education and Assessment in Flinders University, Adelaide, South Australia.

Routledge Contemporary South Asia Series

For the full list of titles in the series please visit: https://www.routledge.com/
Routledge-Contemporary-South-Asia-Series/book-series/RCSA

Empowering Marginalised Women in Remote Indian Villages

An Impact Study

Figure 0.1 A village in the Palni Hills, near Kodaikanal.
Photo by Sethuram on Unsplash. Royalty-free.

Udoy Saikia, Jim Chalmers, Dency Michael, and Janice Orrell

Routledge
Taylor & Francis Group
LONDON AND NEW YORK

First published 2025
by Routledge
4 Park Square, Milton Park, Abingdon, Oxon OX14 4RN

and by Routledge
605 Third Avenue, New York, NY 10158

Routledge is an imprint of the Taylor & Francis Group, an informa business

British Library Cataloguing-in-Publication Data
A catalogue record for this book is available from the British Library

Library of Congress Cataloging-in-Publication Data
Names: Saikia, Udoy, author. | Chalmers, Jim (Associate producer), author. | Michael, Dency, author. | Orrell, Janice, author.
Title: Empowering marginalised women in remote Indian villages : an impact study / Udoy Saikia, Jim Chalmers, Dency Michael, Janice Orrell.
Description: Abingdon, Oxon ; New York : Routledge, 2025. | Series: Routledge contemporary South Asia series | Includes bibliographical references and index.
Identifiers: LCCN 2024030581 (print) | LCCN 2024030582 (ebook) | ISBN 9781032856827 (hardback) | ISBN 9781032856834 (paperback) | ISBN 9781003519409 (ebook)
Subjects: LCSH: Women–India–Tamil Nadu–Social conditions. | Women's rights–India–Tamil Nadu. | Sex discrimination against women–India–Tamil Nadu. | Tamil Nadu (India)–Social conditions.
Classification: LCC HQ1744.T3 S35 2024 (print) | LCC HQ1744.T3 (ebook) | DDC 305.420954/82–dc23/eng/20240708
LC record available at https://lccn.loc.gov/2024030581
LC ebook record available at https://lccn.loc.gov/2024030582

ISBN: 978-1-032-85682-7 (hbk)
ISBN: 978-1-032-85683-4 (pbk)
ISBN: 978-1-003-51940-9 (ebk)

DOI: 10.4324/9781003519409

Typeset in Times New Roman
by Newgen Publishing UK

Contents

Figures

Tables

Acknowledgements

We would like to acknowledge the support and assistance provided by Flinders University College of Social Sciences, Anne Fitzpatrick of the Australian Lutheran World Service, the Jesuit Community at Shenbaganur who have welcomed and given Grihini program space for 37 years and Dency Michael in Kodaikanal.

Glossary

Adivasi refers to heterogeneous tribal groups across the Indian subcontinent. The Constitution of India does not use the word *Adivasi*, instead referring to *Scheduled Tribes* (see separate Glossary entry below).

Backward areas officially designated areas deemed socially, economically, educationally and industrially under-developed; usually pertains to highland and drought-prone areas.

Dalit a name for people belonging to the lowest-stratum castes in India.

Dravidian movement its basis entails three aims: undoing of Brahmin hegemony and religious practices; renewal of Dravidian languages; abolition of caste systems, and transforming women's unequal position in society.

Habitation the smallest level of village settlement in Tamil Nadu; commonly has tens to hundreds of households.

Gross national happiness (GNH) a system of values that guides the government of Bhutan in terms of measuring progress beyond income. It includes an index used to measure the collective happiness and wellbeing of a population. It was developed as a subjective alternative to gross domestic product, which has been used as the orthodox measure of social progress.

Paliyar (or Palaiyar) a grouping of Tribals living in the Southwestern Ghats montane rainforests in South India, especially in Tamil Nadu and Kerala. The Adivasis from AV2 (village in this study) are Paliyar.

Pulaiyar Adivasis from the village designated AV1 in this study.

Scheduled Castes (Dalit)   the official term for Dalits as per the Constitution of India. The term 'Schedule' refers to the legal listing of specific castes in the Indian constitution. For Scheduled Castes (SCs), the criteria involve extreme social, educational and economic deprivation resulting from the practice of untouchability. Currently the Constitution allows only members of Hindu, Sikh and Buddhist religions to be recognised as SCs. The Union government in 2019 rejected the possibility of including Dalit Christians as members of SCs.

Scheduled Tribes   refers to tribal communities or parts of or groups within villages to which an individual belongs by birth (not marriage), conditional on possession of a prescribed certificate of belonging to a community that is included in the Presidential Orders. This is an acute issue for many undocumented people. The term 'Schedule' refers to the legal listing of specific tribes in the Indian constitution.

Sustainable Development Goals (SDGs)   The 2030 Agenda for Sustainable Development agrees on a set of 'Sustainable Development Goals' consisting of 17 goals and 169 targets to try to eradicate poverty and realise a sustainable world.

Taluk   a section of a district in India. It is generally made up of villages that have been organised for economic purposes.

Synopsis of the research

The research focuses on the impacts of social education[1] on the lives of women living in remote mountain villages in Tamil Nadu, India. The analysis quantifies their subjective and objective learning experiences as indicated by wellbeing and empowerment variables, in the contexts of persistent structural inequalities and current public policy that aims to tackle them. While this is a study of wellbeing or quality of life,[2] it adopts an approach and methodology that forge a new pathway. The conceptual grounds centre on the proposition that if there is a gap between measured quality of life and empowerment, then wellbeing is severely weakened by inherent inequalities. That is, only when the gap is closed does wellbeing strengthen. The book investigates this interconnection for its adeptness in uncovering the progress and challenges that rural women face in the struggle for equality. In the case of highland communities in Tamil Nadu, women who identify as either Dalit (lowered caste), Adivasi (tribal) or Sri Lankan Repatriate face racialised and social class inequalities every day. These communities are socially and culturally decreed to occupy the bottom strata of power relations.

In part, literacy disparities account for the worsening of the job situation for marginalised rural women. Even when rural women achieve well educationally, they struggle to avoid being cast in casual, seasonal farm labour jobs. Without more secure and well-paid employment, their wellbeing is critically undermined. At the same time, the women are increasingly resolute in their struggle for social transformation.

The starting point in our approach is recognition that the wellbeing of these rural marginalised women is dependent on access to opportunities. There are scarce job openings, which makes for meagre opportunities to live the life that the women have reason to value. In a state where women are close to gender parity in tertiary education achievements, this implies that education is a necessary but insufficient indicator of wellbeing, in the absence of empowerment.

These conditions are the basis for this study's formulation of variables and indicators that seek to uncover the interconnections between empowerment/decision-making and multiple dimensions of wellbeing. The wellbeing variables are grouped under two headings: capabilities[3] and equalities. 'Capabilities' entail living standard/ livelihoods, physical and mental health, and education. 'Equalities' indicate self-efficacy, social action and human rights.

The conceptual underpinnings draw on the Beijing Declaration and Platform for Action which is the well-established global plan for advancing women's rights. This includes living free from violence, engaging in decisions about her life, having access to similar healthcare and education experiences that men and boys do, and benefiting from opportunities to work on the same footing. The Beijing vision builds on a legacy that includes Mary Wollstonecraft's late 18th-century work titled *A Vindication of the Rights of Woman* (1792). While Wollstonecraft insists that wellbeing and empowerment are inextricably joined in the struggle for equality, it is not until the onset of the 21st century that researchers follow her lead. An example of capability research that does so is Amartya Sen's 1999 work *Development as Freedom* with its recognition that inequalities severely weaken wellbeing.[4] Other work advances this recognition through a focus on empowerment or self-help. Typically, this centres on adult/social education in public spaces where people debate their conditions, examine them and seek mutualising solutions. A leading example in the global south is Paulo Freire's *Pedagogy of the Oppressed*, which has advanced understanding of the intersections of empowerment and social education. The classes of the Grihini programme at Kodaikanal – whose graduates play a central role in our interview process and have experienced a Freirean approach in their social education – are characterised by liberatory content that centres on the women's lived experiences. Grihini College was established as a non-formal education centre in 1987, designed for deprived/vulnerable women living in rural districts of Tamil Nadu. The pedagogy centres on skills in cultural as well as functional literacy, developed through solving everyday problems that women face in their villages.

The measurement system in this research can be traced to the Human Development Report initiative which is set up against orthodox calculations that insist income (gross domestic income / gross domestic product) is the measure of 'progress'. Our methodology is further indebted to Bhutan's Gross National Happiness system, and in turn to the work of the Oxford Poverty and Human Development Initiative (OPHI). These measurement systems are multidimensional and allot equal value to both non-economic and economic aspects of 'progress'. In our case, we draw on a further group of indicators which aim to uncover power relationships that thwart access to opportunities. These are considered alongside indicators of living standard/ livelihoods, health and education.

There are three research goals which arise in the contexts of historical, political, social and cultural oppression of rural women in Tamil Nadu, viz.: 1) to evaluate the impact of empowerment education on the wellbeing of women and their households and villages, with explicit attention to gender equality; 2) to identify and test a theoretical framework that seeks to strengthen studies of wellbeing through a dual focus on capabilities and empowerment – an intersection that shows the progress and the challenges in the struggle for equality that marginalised rural women face; and 3) to investigate the benefits of adult/social education initiatives that support both the development of sustainable livelihoods that match women's skills and training, as well as their participation in village governance.

A set of two different structured questionnaires was administered in five villages to 150 individual women and 150 of the women's household representatives. Two of the villages are predominantly Dalit, two are Tribal, and one is home to Sri Lankan Tamil Repatriates (ex-bonded labourers). About half the women interviewees and their household representatives are graduates of the Grihini programme. Additional focus group discussions (FGDs) took place with a village representative/leader in each of the five villages. FGD participants included two women. The FGDs' aim was to investigate the social or community values or observed benefits/disadvantages of women's empowerment education.

The content of the questionnaires and FGD questions is the result of collaboration with Ms Dency Michael, who is affiliated with the Grihini programme and is located in Kodaikanal. Dency recruited the women's network leaders, who in turn helped to identify the survey sites. Dency also recruited and managed a team of non-Grihini-affiliated field workers, carried out the data entry and collaborated on analysis and the writing of this book. The choice to use convenience sampling was shaped by mitigation policies for the COVID-19 crisis. Convenience sampling recruits interviewees who are available as potential sources of research data. Availability was identified by leaders of the women's network in the region, who assisted in the consent and recruitment process by letting villagers know that we were seeking expressions of interest/consent to engage in interviews.

The findings in this focus book point to the forceful role of social education in women's efforts to achieve equality. Key examples that show up include women's development of livelihood skills that make it possible to avoid cross-generational debt and learn ways to breach damaging traditions like child marriage or forbidden interaction with public officials.

Esther Duflo's 2012 article 'Women Empowerment and Economic Development'[5] helps to situate our findings. Duflo examines two contrasting propositions: 1) development alone could play a major role in driving down inequality between men and women; and 2) empowering women, in terms of decision-making, may benefit development. She asks whether: 1) pushing just one of these two levers would benefit both women's development and their equality; and 2) a focus on women's rights could spark an outcome where women's empowerment and development mutually reinforce each other and women eventually become equal partners in richer societies.

Duflo's concept of 'development' is cast as 'capabilities' in this book and indicated by education achievements, health outcomes and living standard/livelihoods. Additionally, Duflo's concept of 'equality' (indicated by decision-making) is modelled as 'empowerment' in this book (indicated by decision-making, human rights, and confidence and contribution to community life).

The findings in this book corroborate Duflo's conclusion that development (formal education, health and livelihood improvements) is a necessary but insufficient stimulus for equality, while empowerment is contingent on policy actions that favour women. What this book finds is that neither development nor empowerment on their own are sufficient to 'spark equality as the desired outcome'. A conceptual point of difference with Duflo concerns her view that *women's rights* 'will spark an outcome where women's empowerment and development mutually reinforce each other and women eventually become equal partners in richer societies'. Instead, this book argues, it is *social education* rather than *human rights* that is ultimately more consequential. This is because the data on women's rights have become an inherent aspect of governance with an accent on tackling the violations themselves, whereas the basic problem involves *access* to claiming rights. For this reason, the intent in this book is to investigate an unjust status quo and cast light on the political character of administrative actions underlying human rights protocols.

Notes

1 This book uses the term 'adult/social education' in reference to the tradition developed by Maulana Azad, who became India's first Minister of Education following Independence. Maulana Azad renamed the term 'adult education' that existed under British rule, calling it 'social education' to signify its mission of reducing disparities and inequalities through preparing every citizen to play their part in a democratic social order. Maulana Azad strongly advocated the education of women. Source: Relevance of educational philosophy of Maulana Azad (thestatesman.com)
2 It belongs to wellbeing approaches predicated on the multiple dimensions devised by the Gross National Happiness initiative of Bhutan.
3 The capability approach (Sen, Nussbaum, Alkire) is a theoretical framework based on the notion that the freedom to achieve wellbeing is of primary ethical importance, and on a related assertion that wellbeing refers to people's capabilities/achievements and the opportunities that make this possible. Capabilities are further understood as substantive freedoms facilitated by such opportunities.
4 This is also the implication of Mary Wollstonecraft's *A Vindication of the Rights of Woman*.
5 Duflo, Esther (2012). 'Women Empowerment and Economic Development'. American Economic Association (aeaweb.org).

References

Duflo, Esther. Women empowerment and economic development. *Journal of Economic Literature* 50(4), 1051–1079 (2012).
Sen, Amartya. *Development as Freedom* (1st ed.). New York: Oxford University Press (1999).

Warsi, Mohammad J. Relevance of educational philosophy of Maulana Azad. The Statesman. (28 June 2024). www.thestatesman.com/features/releva nce-of-educational-philosphy-of-maulana-azad-1503130101.html

Wollstonecraft, Mary. *A Vindication of the Rights of Woman with Strictures on Political and Moral Subjects.* London: J. Johnson (1792).

1 Scope of an investigation in India of marginalised women's struggle for equality

Introduction

A key context for assessing women's wellbeing and empowerment in Tamil Nadu is the political party system. The Dravidian movement started with the formation of the Justice Party in 1916, in British colonial India.[1] The party represented South Indians (primarily Tamil-speakers) and was established over and against Brahminism's grip on power.[2] The Dravidian movement has persisted to the present day with two political parties now representative of its aims. They have facilitated significant empowerment for marginalised people whose lives are shackled by discrimination, marginalisation, exploitation and deprivation. Signs of progress include the appointment of people from Scheduled Castes as Judges of the Madras High Court in 2020. Earlier gains, in 1982, saw public policy changes that involved the midday meal scheme that was implemented across rural areas. This improved the nutrition, health and education achievements of the poorest people.[3] Their primary health was targeted by other reforms that provided them with subsidised food grains. In education, they benefited from a reform to increase primary school enrolment. This resulted in Tamil Nadu achieving the third-highest primary school enrolment in India. What made this possible was increased public spending and subsidies for members of both Scheduled Castes and Scheduled Tribes.[4] The education reforms almost closed the social strata gap in *primary* educational achievements between Dalits and middle castes. On the other hand, a wide gap involving social strata persists in *higher* levels of education, as discussed later.

While these welfare reforms are significant, Dravidian political parties have not made noteworthy reforms in property redistribution

DOI: 10.4324/9781003519409-1

or tenure. While there was a redistribution of productive assets, this only benefited people with existing access to opportunities.[5] It did not benefit vulnerable social groupings such as Dalits or Tribals/Adivasis. Villages who benefited already had access to subsidies on farm inputs like fertilisers, pesticides and water pumps; and they already had access to microcredit and loan waivers. On the other hand, very few Scheduled Caste and Scheduled Tribe people could benefit because only very rarely do they happen to be middle and large landowners.[6]

In terms of more recent, more progressive public policy actions, civil society leads the way. For example, caste associations have agitated to change caste policies.[7] And Tribal associations affiliated with Parayar, Pallar and Arunthathiyar communities have worked with new minor political parties to 'decriminalise' their communities. Prior to this, their communities had been 'criminalised' by historical Criminal Tribes Acts that 'notified' these communities – acts that were enforced by the British Raj between 1871 and 1947.[8]

The sample populations studied in this research comprise women who self-identify as either 1) Scheduled Caste (Dalit); 2) Sri Lankan Repatriates; 3) Scheduled Tribe (Adivasi, also known as Paliyan or Palaiyar groupings); or 4) 'none of these' (viz. other minoritised community).

Paliyans are included in the List of Scheduled Tribes (Adivasi) in India. They are amongst the earliest settlers or original inhabitants of the Palni Hills. Many Paliyans work as daily-wage labour, engage in beekeeping, cultivate food and sell forest products. The British botanist Nora Mitchell believed these communities were the first builders of hill terraces in these hills[9] (*see cover page photo*). Both Adivasi and Dalit are officially designated among the most disadvantaged socio-economic groups, implying that their efforts to achieve their human potential are systemically blocked by a lack of opportunity to participate.

The Sri Lankan Tamil population in Tamil Nadu encompasses refugees and repatriates who first arrived in India under a two-country agreement for a repatriation scheme. The Tamils had been transported by the British colonial regime to Sri Lanka from southern India in the 19th century. They brought them to work on Sri Lankan hill-country plantations. The larger wave of Sri Lankan Tamils arrived back to India as repatriates in 1983 following the outbreak of the war in Sri Lanka. Upon returning to India many became bonded labourers in India, and some were later granted land in the Palni Hills.

The problem

Lowered Caste, Tribal and Sri Lankan Repatriate women in the high-lands of Tamil Nadu face racialised and social class inequalities every day. These communities have been socially and culturally decreed to occupy the bottom strata of power relations.[10] In the vernacular of capabilities approaches, they are deprived of access to opportunities to jobs, education, healthcare, human rights claims and voice.

At the same time, women are increasingly resolute in the struggle for social transformation. This is evident from choices made to participate in adult/social education, learning how to create and make life choices. There is additional proof in the official statistics on women's high achievements in *tertiary* education.[11] Tamil Nadu has made strong advancements in education. At the same time, there is a gender gap in functional literacy. Recent statistics show that 73.44% of females are literate compared with 86.77% of males.[12]

In part, the literacy disparities account for the worsening of the job situation for marginalised rural women. Even when rural women achieve well educationally, they struggle to avoid being cast in casual, farm labour jobs. Without more secure and well-paid employment, their wellbeing is critically undermined.

Table 1.2 shows the kind of jobs that people have in Dindigul district, which is the key district in this study. More than a third of Dindigul residents are farm labourers who 'work another person's land for cash or kind / share of the crop'. Such work is not constant even if it proceeds 'for a major part of the year'. An additional 35%

Table 1.1 Literacy rates in Tamil Nadu

Female Literacy Rates
While inequality is less visible in Tamil Nadu gender statistics, rural women lag well behind:
Rural women 70.8%; Urban women 85.9%. Indian States by Literacy Rate 2022 | Literacy Rate in India (findeasy.in)
Tamil Nadu state: Female literacy rate: 73.14%, male literacy: 86.77% www.tnenvis.nic.in/Content/Demography_1168.aspx?format=Print#.~:text=Literacy rate in Tamil Nadu,literacy is at 73.14 percent.
Dindigul District: Female literacy: 68.33%, Male literacy: 84.23% Dindigul District Population Census 2011-2022, Tamil Nadu literacy sex ratio and density
DV1 village in Dindigul District: female literacy rate: 61.93%. Male: 81.77%

Table 1.2 Workforce participation, Dindigul district

Source: ^ "Census Info 2011 Final population totals - Dindigul district"	
Main Agricultural Labourers*	34%
Marginal Agricultural Labourers**	5%
Other Workers***	35%
Marginal Workers****	11%
Cultivators*****	13%
Household Industries******	2%

*Worked another person's land for cash or kind/share of crop for a major part of the year

**worked on another person's land for cash or kind/share of crop for less than 6 months in a year

***worked in some non-farming or household industry, e.g., factory workers, plantation workers, mining, construction, teachers, priests, etc.

****worked for less than 6 months in a year in non-farming or household industry, e.g., factory work, plantation work, mining, construction, teachers, priests, etc.

*****engaged as employer, single worker or family worker cultivating land owned/ held from Government or from private person or institution for cash or in kind/ sharing of crops. Cultivators sometimes have some land and also use land belonging to other.

******industry conducted by household head and/or by household members at home or within the village.

of people in Dindigul are 'other workers'. This refers to people who 'worked in some non-farming or household industry, e.g., factory workers, plantation workers, mining, construction, teachers, priests'.

When these job categories are disaggregated by sex, the gender gap in the 'workers' category is 60% male compared to 40% female.[13] There is an almost identical pattern of gender inequity in the category of 'cultivators', with 61% males and 39% females. The gender gap narrows significantly in 'agricultural labourers', with females numbering just under half the total. These employment inequalities represent serious problems that are especially acute for women marginalised by social class and race. Urban people in Tamil Nadu enjoy greater access to jobs. In addition, they possess greater opportunities in education. The prevailing data are clear. The 2017 Human Development Report (HDR) for Tamil Nadu makes recommendations to close the gap in access to secondary and higher secondary schools.[14] The HDR urged state government to take 'the first steps' by improving the availability of schools, classrooms and teachers.[15]

In Tamil Nadu, 30% of habitations[16] have no secondary school within 5 km of their location (the accepted norm). Dindigul (the key district in this study) *has the lowest coverage in the state*. In the case of lowered (Scheduled) Caste habitations in Tamil Nadu, just 13.61% have a local high school. This is lower than the state average for the general population.[17] But even when a habitation *does* have a secondary or higher secondary school, class sizes in rural areas are as high as 59, compared to 35 in urban areas.[18]

Project goals

The intention is to uncover the ramifications for human wellbeing of assumptions baked into neoliberal inequality interventions. Most recently, these interventions are based on 'shared prosperity' through 'opportunity' (to earn money).[19] But the neoliberal discourse ignores the structural inequalities that repress 'opportunity'. This shapes the intention in this book to draw attention to the multidimensionality of 'opportunities', by investigating domains that in addition to living standard include health, education and human rights. This is expected to help clarify some of the critical ways that power impedes access to opportunities. Encapsulating this are the following three research goals, in the contexts of historical, political, social and cultural oppression of rural women in Tamil Nadu:

1) *Evaluate the impact of empowerment education on the wellbeing of women and their households and villages, with explicit attention to gender equality.*
2) *Identify and test an innovative theoretical framework that seeks to strengthen studies of wellbeing through a dual focus on capabilities and empowerment – an intersection that shows the progress*

and the challenges in the struggle for equality that marginalised rural women face.

3) Investigate the benefits of adult/social education initiatives that support both the development of sustainable livelihoods matching women's skills and training, and their participation in village governance.

To reiterate, the guiding image in these aims is that wellbeing is strengthened when it intersects with empowerment. The intersection shows both the progress and the challenges in the struggle for equalities that rural women face, in circumstances where substantive freedoms are severely constrained by lack of access to opportunities.

Significance for global and Indian agendas

The research is expected to support and contribute to the 2030 Global Agenda for Sustainable Development. This refers to the targets in Goal 5 for achieving gender equality and empowering all women and girls (*see Figure 1.1*).

- End all forms of discrimination against all women and girls everywhere.
- Eliminate violence against women and girls in public and private spheres.
- Eliminate harmful practices such as child, early and forced marriage.
- Ensure full participation and equal opportunities for leadership at all levels of decision making.
- Give women equal rights to economic resources, as well as access to ownership and control over land and other forms of property and financial services, inheritance and natural resources.
- Adopt and strengthen enforceable legislation for gender equality and empowerment of women and girls.

Figure 1.1 Targets of Sustainable Development Goal 5: achieve gender equality and empower all women and girls.

The more specific significance for India's policy community is that the study helps to tackle issues that Dalit and Tribal women face regarding their livelihoods, health, education, self-efficacy and human rights.

The study is also expected to help develop research capacity in the villages studied. These villages had direct involvement in the survey methodology and processes: the research engaged women from local villages for data collection, data analysis, interpretation of findings, and writing this book.

Notes

1 The Dravidian Movement entails three foundational aspirational aims: the undoing of Brahmin hegemony and religious practices; the renewal of Dravidian languages, the abolition of caste systems, and transforming women's unequal position in society.
2 More specifically, against speakers of the significantly Sanskrit-based languages of western, northern and parts of eastern India.
3 Subramanian, Narendra (2018) Caste and Social Mobility: Karunanidhi's Dravidian Century (thewire.in).
4 Ibid.
5 Ibid.
6 Ibid.
7 Ibid.
8 Communities that were 'notified' under the reign of the British signified that members of these communities were 'born criminals'. This entailed a series of laws that began with the Criminal Tribes Act of 1871. These Acts were repealed by the Independent Indian Government in 1952, meaning the communities became 'de-notified' (DNTs).
9 A Brief History of the Palani Hills | The Kodai Chronicle.
10 See Jim Chalmers (2001). 'Negations of Caste'. In *Anarcho-Modernism: Toward a New Critical Theory in Honour of Jerry Zaslove*, Vancouver: Talonbooks.
11 Tamil Nadu reportedly had a 49.5% female enrolment compared to a 50.5% male enrolment and a Gender Parity Index of 0.99. Source: AISHE 2019. aishe_eng.pdf (education.gov.in).
12 The India-wide disparity rate is 64.6% for females and 80.9% for males. Source: Shiv Prakash Katiyar (2016). Gender Disparity in Literacy in India. *Social Change* journal. First published February 17, 2016.
13 The data are based on the 2011 census and reported on Dindigul Population (2021/2022), District Taluks List, Tamil Nadu (indiagrowing.com).

14 Government of Tamil Nadu. State Planning Commission. Tamil Nadu State Human Development Report – 2017 State Planning Commission (tn. gov.in).
15 Ibid.
16 Habitations are the smallest level of village settlement that commonly have tens to hundreds of households.
17 Tamil Nadu State Human Development Report – 2017 p. 95.
18 Ibid. p. 96.
19 The 'Shared Prosperity' myth is advanced by the World Bank platform to tackle inequality. For a comprehensive critique, see Shane Chalmers and Sundhya Pahuja, 'The Inequity of Development: Reading the World Bank's Turn to Inequality', in Antony Anghie, Bhupinder Chimni, Michael Fakhri, Karin Mickelson and Vasuki Nesiah (eds), *Handbook of Third World Approaches to International Law* (Edward Elgar, forthcoming).

References

Census India. *Census Info 2011 Final population totals – Dindigul district.* Dindigul District Population Census 2011 - 2021 - 2024, Tamil Nadu literacy sex ratio and density

Chalmers, Jim. 'Negations of Caste'. In Ian Angus (ed.), *Anarcho-Modernism: Toward a New Critical Theory in Honour of Jerry Zaslove*, pp. 243–256. Vancouver: Talonbooks (2001).

Chalmers, Shane, and Sundhya Pahuja, 'The Inequity of Development: Reading the World Bank's Turn to Inequality'. In Antony Anghie, Bhupinder Chimni, Michael Fakhri, Karin Mickelson and Vasuki Nesiah (eds.), *Handbook of Third World Approaches to International Law*. Edward Elgar (forthcoming).

Government of India, Ministry of Education. All India Survey on Higher Education (AISHE) (2020). www.education.gov.in/sites/upload_files/mhrd/files/statistics-new/aishe_eng.pdf

Government of Tamil Nadu. State Planning Commission. Tamil Nadu State Human Development Report – 2017 State Planning Commission (tn.gov.in).

India Growing. Dindigul Population. District Taluks List, Tamil Nadu (indiagrowing.com) (2021/2022).

Katiyar, Shiv Prakash. Gender Disparity in Literacy in India. *Social Change Journal*, 46(1), (2016). DOI:10.1177/0049085715618558

Subramanian, Narendra. 'Caste and Social Mobility: Karunanidhi's Dravidian Century' (thewire.in) (2018).

Vasanth, Nishita. 'A Brief History of the Palani Hills'. *The Kodai Chronicle.* Oct. 30, 2021. www.thekodaichronicle.com/community/a-brief-history-of-the-palani-hills

2 Rationale for including inequality in women's wellbeing approaches

The explanatory force of wellbeing approaches

This section deepens and broadens understanding of how wellbeing approaches advance investigations of empowerment or agency by situating the authors' approach alongside the measurement systems to which it is indebted, and conversely, setting it against the method it sets out to supplant. The forerunners of this wellbeing approach are the 'human development' or 'capability' paradigm together with its recent manifestations driven by the Gross National Happiness (GNH) initiative, whereas the system they contest is the longstanding tradition of assessing 'progress' on the sole basis of gross national income (GNI) or gross domestic product (GDP).

Looking first at the convention of using GNI/GDP metrics to measure 'human progress', this idea is associated with the 'Washington Consensus'. The Consensus came about when Washington-based officials agreed on a global set of ends and means intended to inform the work of development practitioners and analysts. Other words that are interchangeable with Washington Consensus include: 'economic orthodoxy', 'neoliberalism', 'free trade', 'new world order' and 'late capitalism'.

Increasingly, a shift away from the GNI approach can be seen. Evidence for this stems from various events that include: 1) the disaffection of a key economist associated with the Washington Consensus, Joseph Stiglitz[1]; 2) the establishment of commissions of state inquiries into people's lack of wellbeing[2]; 3) the preparation of the World Happiness Report[3]; 4) the incompatibility of a sole GNI measure with mounting inequalities; and 5) the High-Level Meeting on Wellbeing and Happiness at the United Nations Headquarters in 2012. This UN

DOI: 10.4324/9781003519409-2

meeting featured a presentation by a small member state, Bhutan, of its GNH initiative.[4] Bhutan announced its system of measurement in terms of a 'new paradigm'. It explained how this method gives prominence to subjective components of 'progress' alongside the more familiar objective metrics. The subjective indicators assess people's satisfaction with social inclusion and their quality of access to social goods (education, healthcare).

The assessment of people's satisfaction with the allocations of benefits from social goods is always about more than just economic matters. The key point which Bhutan's GNH manifests and which the orthodox economics of GNI disregards is that 'progress' is primarily about access to opportunities and choices; and at policy level this necessitates inclusive policy attitudes about welfare that include but go beyond 'standard of living'. Deciding on the exact nature of such policies and attitudes is among the greatest challenges that a country faces for immediate and long-term progress.

The exact model of assessing the costs/benefits of development that fit a particular country or sub-national state will vary, but in all cases the end goal is concern for the plight of the most vulnerable individuals. This is vital and puts emphasis firmly on access to opportunities as opposed to abstract opportunities.

As mentioned, recognition of the inaptness of GNI has grown in extent and intensity in recent times, including within neoliberal circles. It is useful to elaborate on the series of consequential events noted above. The first of these was in 2008 when neoliberal French President Sarkozy established the Commission on the Measurement of Economic Performance and Social Progress. Notably, Sarkozy chose dissident neoliberal economist Joseph Stiglitz to lead the Commission alongside Amartya Sen and Jean-Paul Fitoussi. The Commission's aim was to improve the existing measurement system by investigating the value of wellbeing approaches. The wellbeing approach they developed was a significant step away from the maxims of late capitalism. However, what they did *not* do was consider the ultimate goals of human progress and the specific collective actions needed for societies to be able to advance people's wellbeing. But at least they questioned the sustainability of human progress as presently imagined. In other words, they were highly sceptical of the orthodox notion that what people are able to do with their lives is solely predicated on their economic resources. The problem they saw with this is that it assumes infinite growth of economic resources in an environment that is finite.

The second event in these departures from orthodoxy involves the report commissioned by David Cameron's Conservative UK government's Sustainable Development Commission. Like its Sarkozy antecedent, this Commission also relied on an unorthodox economic advisor, Tim Jackson, who headed the Commission. His progressive book *Prosperity without Growth*[5] was originally published as a report to the Conservative UK government. In essence the Jackson report took up the same theme as the Sarkozy Commission, namely that prosperity will soon be impossible because of unsustainable assumptions about GNI growth. Conversely, it understood that prosperity and wellbeing *are* possible if the endless pursuit of GNI growth is reined in.

The above two events are significant when considering the supplanting of the orthodox measuring system and its replacement with a wellbeing model. A third event involving Bhutan's GNH contributes much more. This event took place on 2 April 2012 when the United Nations implemented Resolution 65/309. The Resolution had previously been adopted by the General Assembly in July 2011 under the title 'Happiness: towards a holistic approach to development'. In 2012 the UN pointedly placed wellbeing or quality of life on the global development agenda. Key speakers at the 2012 General Assembly event included Joseph Stiglitz and also Jeffrey Sachs, who used the occasion to launch his *World Happiness Report*.[6] He had previously featured in a global conference hosted by Bhutan. Meanwhile, in the most significant of its various influences on the paradigm shift, Bhutan produced its second GNH report in 2010, an event that piqued the interest of development theorists and practitioners, including the authors of this book.

Since the early 1970s, neoliberal economists had been telling development specialists that the categories of development are essentially based on a few quantitative indicators of 'progress'. Typically, these indicators measure living standards and health, using income in the first instance and freedom from chronic diseases in the second. Certainly, chronic diseases (heart disease, stroke, cancer, chronic respiratory diseases and diabetes) are the primary cause of global mortality, but as foundational measures of human *progress* they lack explanatory power. They tell us nothing about the richness (or lack thereof) of human relationships and vitality of human spirit. These qualitative data shortcomings had become evident to growing numbers of researchers. They had seen the statistics where humans generally are living longer and wealthier lives yet suffering qualitatively. The GNI metric neglected what most people wanted policymakers to tackle.

Most people would instantly put income inequality as the everyday inequality they have to deal with in their own lives. A question this raises about measurement systems for the workplace is that a broader jobs lens is needed. Instead of analysing the issue as 'employment', it is more accurate to see the issue as 'people and their work or livelihoods'. Do the resulting jobs reduce their poverty? If so, in what ways? Are the effects similar for women? Do they positively influence dignity, and if so, how? How does employment influence women's social inclusion and participation in political, community and cultural life? Do jobs that raise women's earnings also improve their discretionary spending on food, health and education, and improve their bargaining power at home? All of these questions have implications for making a better roadmap for progress because they interrogate both the cause and the end goal.

While income inequality is just one of the core aspects of multidimensional inequality, its impact is increasingly bad. This is seen in India in a headline that reads 'Income inequality has doubled in 20 years'.[7] Wage disparities are a main trigger of income inequality in India, but when inequalities are viewed in terms of distributive justice the issue is not fully explained by income inequalities. Instead, as shown by multidimensional research such as this one, disparities in access and in the quality of certain key services between rich and poor are key reasons for inequalities in education achievements, healthcare and social protection.

Claims are often heard that income poverty has decreased and income disparities are improving. But these claims rely on GNI aggregate measurements. When disaggregated by gender, the statistics show that 'one in every 10 women is living in extreme poverty (10.3%). If current trends continue, by 2030, an estimated 8% of the world's female population – 342.4 million women and girls – will still be living on less than $2.15 a day'.[8]

In India, assessments in which disaggregation is able to capture the complexities of multidimensional inequalities uncover the challenges that rural villages face. Rural people often live in what are ostensibly healthier natural environments compared to urban dwellers. However, they invariably have poor access to education, healthcare and many social protection services. Urban dwellers are relatively better off in this regard. They often have access to health and education. On the other hand, their deprivations and vulnerability lie in other dimensions like overcrowded unsafe houses, insecure neighbourhoods, unhygienic conditions, noise and air pollution, traffic congestion and more. In short, absolute standards of living uncovered by GNI metrics tell us very little about multidimensional inequalities that occur between social classes, women and men, urban and rural areas.

In its essential formations and consequences, the problem of inequalities is the problem of affordable access to resources and power. Since an individual's wellbeing is interdependent with the group's relative wellbeing, whenever a social grouping (e.g., Dalits, Adivasi, or Sri Lankan Repatriates) experiences discrimination or exclusion, individual wellbeing is adversely affected. Frances Stewart captures this in her concept of horizontal inequalities.[9] Her central idea is that vertical inequality only reveals a single dimension where individuals are split off from one another through income inequality, whereas the concept of *horizontal* inequalities explains how and why this happens. It accounts for the multiple dimensions (class, gender, age, ethnicity, caste, language, practices of belief) through which one community is split from others. This involves systematic, structural ways that block access to opportunities.

The wellbeing that a person could achieve is dependent on the social facilities that transfer potentially empowering conditions. These conditions encompass emotional, psychological and physical health, and basic education, as well as economic opportunities and political freedoms to pursue them. The nature and conditions of employment impact on wellbeing, and there are significant differences along gender lines. This is why a roadmap for eliminating inequalities needs to consider not just variations in availability and access, but also whether access is guaranteed with equity, non-discrimination and dignity.

Global inequalities are experienced differently in different places by different social groupings. Household estimates do not usually uncover the variations within the household. However, when there is this focus, it shows that women and girls are more affected than men and boys. For example, in households that suffer hunger due to poor access to scarce resources, women and girls often eat less food and get less healthcare than the men and boys in that household. The extent of the gap between the sexes varies across cultures and time. A key variable is ownership of assets. Reportedly, women own less than 20% of the world's land.[10] Moreover, in the rare cases where women do enjoy land rights, they have often been appropriated when land use is transformed to facilitate export production. This impels women into farm labour and the lowest-paid manufacturing jobs.

Power and inequalities

In large part, social systems historically reproduce and renew inequality on the basis of decision-making in society. Globally, women's voices are very poorly represented at all levels and especially in sub-national sites. Further, the legal system typically discriminates against women in family law, inheritance, property and land ownership, citizenship and criminal law, where prosecution of violence against women is particularly difficult. The obvious question this raises is how to transform paradigmatic structures that institutionalise gender inequalities. The goal of such interventions needs to be deepening understanding and building demand for access to material assets, land title and voice – challenges that have been taken up by the field of social education. These struggles can be grouped under the headings of distributive justice and the right to wellbeing. The right to wellbeing and distributive justice encompass dimensions that are hidden by an economics driven by GNI analysis. Such approaches conceal the historical narratives of people's attempts to attain wellbeing. These alternative narratives show that access to opportunities to realise wellbeing is typically constrained by difficult healthcare conditions, unequal opportunities to gain knowledge, and workplace conditions that deplete human dignity. In other words, measurement systems able to improve distributive justice need to be focused on subjects and not on objects of development. This implies that recognition of people's rights should be as both individuals and members of a community.

The challenge of distributive justice is hindered by traditional methodologies. The starting point in such methods typically involves making a roadmap, which is not a problem in itself; it is simply the wrong place to start. The first thing to figure out is *where* to go to. The route is not the problem; rather, it is knowing where to try to get to. The inference in traditional approaches is that the destination is a given. It is prescribed by the assumption of advancing infinite growth in labour productivity. Against this assumption, as proponents of distributive justice Amartya Sen and Martha Nussbaum insist, practitioners need to base their roadmaps on recognition that the end goal is the actualisation of human potential. This makes material wealth the important means to achieve this – but not the goal itself. Their insights reflect evidence that 'poverty improvements' over the last 20 years have not transferred sustainable progress for all people. Inequalities persist and reproduce for minoritised social groupings. Moreover, there is clear evidence of systemic, institutionalised inequalities. Empirical expression of distributive injustice is found in an important Human Development Report (HDR) which encompasses 20 years of HDR research[11]. The 2010 report notes that disparities are soaring in income and consumption of goods and services, in years of schooling and in health outcomes.

Significantly, the 2010 HDR refers to additional unexamined inequalities. These emerge in specific dimensions of deprivation – those that the HDR measurement system is still not yet designed to investigate due to their need for consistent data across all countries. Nonetheless, the HDR signalled the need for these inequality data, and shortly afterwards, the challenge was taken up by wellbeing approaches. Their heuristic value lay in the intent and ability to tackle the big questions ('progress?') while simultaneously advancing the systems of measurement.

Orthodox measurement systems are dependent on outputs and results at an aggregate level. This tells policymakers very little about what has worked and what has failed at community levels (let alone within households). Addressing this is a crucial underpinning of wellbeing approaches, in responding to demands by policymakers. Globally the policy community is under enormous pressure by donors and treaty bodies to measure and track government performance subnationally. This sets up heavy demands on policymakers to provide community-level explanations which, in turn, rely on the availability of wellbeing metrics that can be decomposed to see what policies work or fail for stratified social groupings.

While GDP and GNI were not originally intended to measure human progress, this did become the normative proxy of 'progress'. Their original intention was just to count the money value of all goods and services that a country produces. The problem of GNI that persists today is that it carries an implication of wellbeing or progress, even though this was never intended to be the case.

In the world of orthodox metrics, productivity growth consists of gross values. They do not include net values like those added by social education, social skills, group memberships, human rights, voice and participation in civic affairs. Increasingly, researchers have seen that counting gross values deeply discounts and bypasses household duties like taking care of dependents, which are considered non-economic by the orthodoxy. Neither does GNI measure family and community cohesion, nor an individual's inner states and dignity. Consequently, the traditional measurement system is indifferent to how a household sometimes gets richer yet remains worse off, in terms of time poverty for example, where time poverty of parents creates pressure points in respect to nutrition and other essential forms of dependents' nourishment.

The imperative for measurement approaches is to investigate power imbalance in relation to autonomy or agency. This challenge implies addressing socio-cultural barriers that impede participation by women and other minoritised social groupings in socio-political life. Traditional economic reasoning can be reduced to a claim that equal rights for women are merely a precondition for increased productivity and market growth. This constitutes a narrow focus on labour productivity. Yet there is ample evidence that employed women spend an excessive amount of work time on the double burden of paid work plus home duties. Counting unpaid work, women's total work hours are longer than men's in all regions of the world.[12] The dominant economic theory is incompatible with consequences of late capitalism that show girls too are working longer hours than boys, whether on housework only, employment only, or both. Further, girls' school attendance declines as the number of hours spent on household duties increases, and consequently, lack of education impacts on teen marriages in ways that include dangerous health impacts of early childbearing, in contexts that notably include lack of access to clean water.

Globally, most people still live in rural households – at least for now. Most are integrated into the global market economy, but the measure of productivity growth fails to capture the significant thing of what they contribute productively and the costs of their productivity. The reason for this failing is that the market economy is merely a part of rural people's stories; most people have other economies that they participate in as well.[13] For example, all rural peoples are in a household economy, usually to a large extent, yet there is no recording of productivity in the GNI system which reflects these fuller linkages. This means that inequality is very much underestimated at global, national and sub-national levels. For example, the core metric of GNI shows disinterest in gender inequalities due to a preoccupation with labour growth. This averts focus away from broader productivity growth that women create in multiple sites like relationships and community, as well as household productivity. The orthodox measures of 'development' leave many women very vulnerable to exploitation. It becomes visible, for instance, in how industrialisation requires vast areas of subsistence lands for export crop production. In cases where appropriation tends to push women into farm labour, or many others into the lowest-paid manufacturing jobs, it has the additional effect of renewing structural barriers that many women face in relation to knowledge opportunities and networks of power.

Amartya Sen understood that productivity growth should enable human flourishing in historical conditions of power inequities. It should not operate as the end goal. He acknowledged causal links between productivity growth and improved quality of life but saw how they are contingent on the ways in which increased income is used socially to combat power imbalance. He had seen how India was failing to use its higher income well in terms of spending on social sector improvements (when compared with Bangladesh).[14]

The search for indicators

To be able to effectively tackle inequalities, policymakers need complex measurements that encompass a focus on local social sectors. This means sub-indicators that enable identification and analysis of pressure points. These include variables such as voice, decision-making and human rights – all by gender differences.

There is a broad consensus concerning a need for multidimensional measures at sub-national levels, but that consensus is much less at individual and subjective levels and more at household level in terms of objective determinants. This is because mathematical economists are uneasy about subjective measures. To try to counter this, the UNDP presented a next-generation set of indices in 2010.[15] While that new system persisted with objective determinants, it did so in the form of a Multidimensional Poverty Index (MPI) as well as a Gender Inequality Index (GII) that is also multidimensional.

A closer look at the GII shows it is a composite statistic that measures three dimensions of vulnerability or deprivation: reproductive health, empowerment and participation (labour market and political voice). As a unitary measure, the index identifies links between gender inequality and a country's loss of achievement, which can be traced to inequality in the capability dimensions of health, education and income. If a country scores a higher index value, this means there is a higher correlation of deprivation across the three dimensions. In other words, increases in the index refer to cross-dimensional interconnections between deprivations. For social analysis this means that the GII can be used to specify and help explain broader and deeper impacts of a specific deprivation. The mathematical basis for this deduction is the probability that inequalities in the included dimensions impact on one another adversely in both directions. For example, a two-way effect shows up between inequality in schooling, maternal mortality and access to work opportunities, among other variables.

The logic of the GII ensures that if a country shows a low achievement in one dimension, its global ranking is not totally compensated for by high achievement in another. The idea is that prognostics should be focused on systemic disadvantages or 'unfreedoms'. What this word means here is that people who are deprived of opportunities to enjoy wellbeing consequently experience 'unfreedom'.

The multiple and multiplying factors of unfreedom are captured in the MPI of the HDR system. The MPI surpasses income-based poverty measures (GNI) by uncovering the manifold deprivations that people face, while simultaneously confronting money shortage. The MPI index contains recognition that deprivation is more than just being income-poor: a person who is 'MPI-poor' is defined as facing multiple deprivations all at once in education, health and all other aspects of living standards besides income. The MPI system selects three dimensions – living standards, health and education – because firstly they are countable, secondly they can be estimated with official data that enable comparison across country contexts, and thirdly they contain simplicity. The latter is considered a virtue of message-making when it is aimed at influencing policymaking.

In Bhutan's search for indicators that uncover distributive injustice, that country set out on a distinctive path. It had previously carried out preliminary attempts to prepare a GNH system in 2006. At that time the Centre for Bhutan Studies developed a very comprehensive survey tool comprising 1500 variables across 11 dimensions of objective plus subjective wellbeing. The survey comprised four priority areas. They were defined to help create policy conditions that could enable every citizen to pursue happiness with a reasonable chance of success. The 'four pillars' were: sustainable and equitable socio-economic development; conservation of environment; preservation and promotion of culture; and promotion of governance.

In the subsequent GNH survey that resulted in the 2010 GNH, Bhutan produced a unitary measure that recognises the correlation between the achievement of wellbeing and having individual agency (the capacity to act in the world). A crucial dimension of this relationship is a mutualistic commitment to act on concern for the wellbeing of others. Bhutan defined 'acting on collective concern' in terms of individual capabilities allied with duty-bearer accountabilities, and they measured this across nine dimensions. These dimensions comprise bodily health (physical, psychological/emotional wellbeing), education, governance, standard of living, use of time, cultural diversity and resilience, community vitality and environmental diversity. Importantly, the nine dimensions are inalienable and indivisible. The guiding idea is that social education and knowledge, for instance, cannot be split from physical, psychological and emotional health, nor from governance, cultural diversity and resilience, community vitality, or environmental diversity. For instance, the purpose of schooling goes beyond producing functional literacy, or even critical thinking (viewed as an abstract quality); there are explicit other social education goals like enhancing cultural diversity and human resilience in the face of climate change and urbanisation. Similarly, a private enterprise is intended to serve a social function by raising living standards through jobs. However, it could and should do much more; and in order to be consistent with and promote wellbeing, a private enterprise would need to promote physical and emotional wellbeing and advance social goals and environmental health.

The indicators in the GNH and in subsequent approaches, like this one that draw on its system, identify various indicators in each dimension that is studied. For example, in education/knowledge, this typically means estimating achievements by: 1) level of education attained; 2) literacy rate; 3) proficiency in mother tongue; and 4) historical literacy (knowledge of local legends and folk stories, local or indigenous knowledge systems). These achievements are then viewed alongside obstacles to education such as access to quality education. Such indicators cover personal, collective and relational variables. This mix transfers recognition that wellbeing consists of multiple interconnected and complementary factors, and that they work in two-way directions. While this is the same objective formulated by the MPI capabilities model, Bhutan's approaches to wellbeing encompass *three additional analytical dimensions*: environment, culture and psychological/emotional wellbeing.

Context is a crucial part of the value of a measurement system capable of revealing how and why a person could be deprived of wellbeing. In other words, the indicators that comprise wellbeing survey questions are context-specific because the ultimate goal is to isolate systemic disadvantages. The search for indicators involves combining subjective *processes* with *outcomes* at the subjective level. In turn, the search combines comprehensive subjective indicators with outcomes at the objective level, for example an indicator of self-reported health status. Typically, this might be in response to a question that asks the number of days that a respondent had been sick or incapacitated.

Turning to the *uses* of wellbeing indicators, the ultimate value for analysis involves a unitary measure of wellbeing (an index) derived from the indicators. The unitary measure enables researchers to observe multiple dimensions while evaluating the effects of all variables on responses of special interest. This is a kind of 'cluster analysis', which can be contrasted with 'high-level analysis' where interest is reduced to statistics that observe strata within a particular dimension. An example of high-level analysis would be the case of a particular dimension such as psychological wellbeing, where observation is limited to the following kinds of variables: distribution of people by wellbeing, mean wellbeing by sex and stratum (e.g., rural–urban), by district, age, educational attainment, occupation, household size, health status, number of people one can count on if having financial problems, number of people one can count on if sick, etc. High-level analysis is severely limited by the fact that it transfers an assumption that there is a 'single big underlying cause'. This is problematic in itself but it also avoids questions of systemic disadvantages – neglecting such factors as income-poor people being unable to afford to pay the costs of transport to school, as an important example.

Wellbeing approaches transfer recognition that there is no single big cause, which means that systemic disadvantages matter. Across a range of dimensions, wellbeing indicators are identified on the ability to capture outcomes and shortages. In terms of shortages, there is a processual component to indicators that seeks answers to questions like 'how it feels to experience ill health and then have to face the reality of irregular or unaffordable public transport'. To further appreciate this point, assume that for a particular person, education/ knowledge is a pressure point for her lack of wellbeing. (Note that wellbeing approaches allow for a particular dimension like education to be readily identified). In cases where education is a key driving force, the measurement system enables this to be probed further in terms of sub-indicators. This exercise could well uncover a catalyst such as low satisfaction with service provision, for example.

To consider another example, assume that the problem of 'lack of wellbeing' boils down to psychological variables, and that indicators point to 'educated unemployment' as an issue of special interest. Being able to isolate the latter variable of interest has the positive effect of catalysing further analysis. This enables better understanding of multiple pressure points. In this particular case, the analysis could prompt a further database search for such information as whether a woman has people that she can count on if having financial problems, or whether she has difficulty in accessing education services.

Such examples help to show how wellbeing approaches enable researchers to present policymakers with a much more comprehensive picture of vulnerability. In short, it is a clear advantage over GNI calculations to have individual-level data rather than those at household level. At the same time, wellbeing approaches should not be seen as an unqualified blueprint. Instead, they contain principles from which researchers can determine usefulness by testing the approach against the historical specifics of a population. Such specifics show up in power relationships that damage the lives of people who are socially excluded – such as Dalits, Adivasi and Sri Lanka Repatriates in this research. In sum, the design of composite measures should reflect the comprehensive wellbeing of individuals and their villages since inequality is not just about being income-poor.

The test of a wellbeing approach is the ability of its indicators to show which interventions work (or do not) for the most vulnerable groups. This is the benchmark of sufficiency. Indicators need to be able to determine the impact of a particular intervention in terms of how different individuals experience it. Note how this makes the wellbeing approaches with which this book is aligned definitively different to hedonic 'happiness' systems. Logically the latter approach makes narcissism the implied goal, and such logic simply resembles the economic orthodoxy, in that it originates in a spurious goal and is then followed by attempts to measure humans as alienated objects of development.

To emphasise a previous observation, *contexts* are a critical aspect of the search for indicators. Context here implies the importance of assessing the possible range of different people's responses to challenges of wellbeing and resistance to the traumas that they encounter. When trying to identify meaningful indicators, this means reflecting on how different cultures develop specific ways to express responses to possible survey questions. This can be traced to the realities of different concepts of moral beliefs and ensuing social orders. In the search for indicators, this implies that people can be expected to show infinitely different responses to survey questions in different country contexts.

While wellbeing presupposes an ethical response or set of actions, the *kind* of ethos is distinct to specific societies. For example, while dignity is essentially linked to rightness and wrongness, this is universal but not absolute. In some societies dignity becomes wrapped in honour and duty. In such cases dignity shows up in a derivative form (honour or duty). The reasons for this need to be investigated in the search for indicators. Useful studies include the work of early anthropologist Ruth Benedict and other students of Franz Boas at Colombia University. Their approach was to analyse different social practices in relation to 'typical customs' that reproduce ritualised responses. A ritualised response to questions that probe dignity, for example, could mean that a traumatic situation produces shame rather than feelings of indignity. The Boas School transfers an important emphasis to the search for indicators: namely, each culture has its own moral imperatives, and they can shape radically different responses. This emphasis on cultural variability is visible in Ruth Benedict's 1946 study of Japanese society, *The Chrysanthemum and the Sword*.[16] Its relevance relates to explaining situations where governance (social contract) is based on individuals choosing what is expected and where dissent is unpatriotic.

Where personal desires for wellbeing are subsumed by collective expectations, this ostensibly contradicts but might operate as the *counterpart* of wellbeing ideals. This occurs whenever individuals choose what is best for human flourishing in terms of the social good. On the other hand, it is vital to anticipate that in some societies a vulnerable person might hesitate to disclose a lack of wellbeing. This is not because they feel they have done something wrong to cause their lack of wellbeing; rather, they might hesitate to acknowledge it because a particular hierarchy of norms impels them to put social honour ahead of the value that personal economic and social status are important.

In terms of investigating dignity, in studies of discriminated populations, it is worth repeating that the challenge of developing measures of subjective wellbeing involves recognition that dignity is a universal rather than an absolute. That is, the determinants of dignity (or indignation) are contextual. While researchers could accurately anticipate the ability of respondents to distinguish the intrusion of cultural imperatives on their authentic thoughts or feelings, this might not be explicit in self-reported survey responses. This carries specific complexities for training survey enumerators and for undertaking the focus groups as a complementary and validating part of the wellbeing survey system.

The idea that individuals could have 'double strategies' is perhaps evident on the strength of the 1903 work of African American rights activist and sociologist William DuBois.[17] He examined strategies for survival that African Americans worked out, and he saw that they reflect a dynamic process involving internal ethoi and external sanctions. Ultimately the latter will differ in different societies, yet the variation highlights the need to explore the specificity of sanctions. Sometimes, as Paolo Freire has done in Brazilian contexts, there have been efforts to universalise the notion of double strategies. But while his resulting idea of a 'culture of silence' is suggestive, it is unlikely to be universal in ways that could shape the search for indicators. This is because double strategies make the job of identifying subjective-level indicators challenging wherever collective identity is more important than subjective facts.

Collectively taken, the above examples show that self-reported 'lack of wellbeing' has the potential to imply a source of unspoken shame. It does not mean that it will be so in all country contexts, but it could be. And the latter could imply a take-away message that only if one has effectively hidden something like domestic violence has one preserved one's dignity. So, again, the challenge of a search for indicators at subjective levels is complicated by expectations that some respondents could be defensive about dignity or not admit to a lack of indignation. Selection and analysis of indicators need to be able to encompass these and other situations. For example, in some social settings, vulnerable persons might not want to stand out and be noticed by oppressive authorities. Another scenario concerns settings where there is a normativising of household violence. This would mean a need to anticipate signs of reluctance to disclose true social status because survival in situations of upheaval and danger requires a special kind of logic. This could mean that resilience is enhanced by hiding awareness so that one is not noticed.

Regarding possible stigmatisation being associated with lack of wellbeing, the work of 20th-century sociologist Erving Goffman is relevant. He was interested in stigma being directed at the gap between what a person could be and what a person actually is. For example, an income-poor woman is unlikely to be able to pay bribes and 'voluntary' costs (where non-payment reflects badly on civic duty), where these are essential to gain access to quality services at school. Note again that the defining quality of wellbeing indicators is 'goal-oriented', since ultimately an indicator is the measure of an aim and its contexts. As already mentioned, the aim is a priori in the sense of coming before the selection of the indicators. The intent to measure wellbeing becomes the basis for choosing the indicators. The indicators would not be chosen primarily because they investigate distribution of opportunities, for instance. They are chosen because they enhance the aim to measure and analyse wellbeing in vulnerable populations.

Essentially, good indicators will have links to success criteria of interventions that are designed on people's behalf, rather than designed for the purpose of identifying productivity gains. Again, the best wellbeing indicators encompass processes pertaining to access to opportunities. Dignity and respect are instrumental aspects of access. Conceptually, this is a factor of systemic relationships related to governance. Indicators need to be able to show this in regard to distributive justice. Nancy Fraser argues for this kind of conceptualisation through key indicators that are focused on recognition (respect).[18] Lack of recognition is typically found in sites such as frontline service providers, where the hierarchy of status breeds disrespect for others in contexts of stratification. In the search for indicators, this implies that variables should not reduce the social to the subjective level, and vice versa. In regard to investigating access to public goods, it means choosing indicators that can uncover non-affordable access at the levels of both sociality and subjectivity. At the level of sociality or institutionalised organisational hierarchies, the indicators need to encompass such actions as disrespect and blocked access, while in terms of subjectivity this implies identifying variables that indicate a 'drive for recognition or dignity' to help the analyst identify acts of status subordination.

Another useful resource in the search for indicators that point up the importance of recognition (voice and power) is the 'Voices of the Poor' project.[19] It comprises three books presenting the experiences of more than 60,000 income-poor women and men in 73 countries. What is suggestive concerning the search for indicators is its analysis focused on process freedoms. Both Amartya Sen and Joseph Stiglitz present analyses in that project. Their insights show the importance of recognition (voice and power) in the ways that deprived people define their dignity (or lack thereof). Other researchers in the 'Voices' study emphasise the differences in how women and men prioritise different things in their striving for dignity. Regarding the search for wellbeing indicators, this accentuates the importance of attention to 'hierarchies of priorities' and the differences and contexts that these hierarchies point to.

To summarise this discussion of the searches for wellbeing indicators, the predicate is the aim to uncover a blend of the following: systemic barriers to access; gaps in wellbeing; and efforts at creative adaptation. The result can be seen in the image that signatures of wellbeing are rooted in dignity or empowerment yet must often endure and respond to shameful conditions of oppression and humiliation. To come up with indicators able to capture this dynamic quality as well as blend the social and subjective dimensions requires a dialectical model. Indicators need to be able to investigate the dialectic between internally autonomous ethical principles and externally imposed sanctions. The former are associated with authentic notions of dignity while the latter involve responses to normative (inauthentic) valorisation of values like honour, duty and reputation. The comprehensive effect of dynamic approaches (shared purpose) is contained in the idea of a universal if contextualised will to persist towards realisation of wellbeing. The 'Voices' project shows this as the shared intent of respondents to understand what causes their deprivations.

Another way of saying this is that indicators need to be framed in ways that enable better understanding of the different ways in which individuals and villages construct belonging. This refers to recognition that social organisation transfers different forms of stratification that integrate a few individuals and villages into networks of power and prosperity and exclude or marginalise most others. Indicators that investigate processes of belonging (social self-identification) need to reflect exclusion that blends with aspiration for dignity/recognition and participation. The hunt for indicators needs to be further informed by ethics of universal justice and expansion of local choices. In studies of inequalities in rural sites, the variables need to particularly represent the distinct choices of women and girls as members of minoritised social groupings.

In the final instance, vulnerable or deprived people are generally doing their best to achieve wellbeing in the circumstances, so that essentially 'wellbeing' is an unfinished project. For this reason, wellbeing variables go through infinite transformations over time. Yet the key factor that remains in the search for indicators is the aim to improve access to opportunities for the realisation of wellbeing.

Notes

1 With specific reference to his 2002 book *Globalization and its Discontents*. W.W. Norton & Company.
2 The Sarkozy Commission and the UK Happiness Index under David Cameron.
3 By Jeffrey Sachs, creator of the Millennium Development Goals.
4 The full title is The Report of the High-Level Meeting on Wellbeing and Happiness Defining a New Economic Paradigm. 2 April 2012. United Nations Headquarters. New York. Available at 617BhutanReport_WEB_F.pdf (un.org).
5 Tim Jackson (2009). *Prosperity without Growth. Foundations for the Economy of Tomorrow*. Routledge.
6 Jeffrey Sachs is economist, public policy analyst, and former director of The Earth Institute at Columbia University. In 2012, he was nominated for World Bank leadership.
7 *The Times of India* announced this in its 7 December 2011 edition.
8 UN Women Facts and figures: Economic empowerment | UN Women – Headquarters.
9 Frances Stewart (2008). *Horizontal Inequalities and Conflict. Understanding Group Violence in Multiethnic Societies*. Palgrave Macmillan, London.
10 World Economic Forum. Women own less than 20% of the world's land. It's time to give them equal property rights | World Economic Forum (weforum.org)
11 See 2010 Human Development Report titled 'The Real Wealth of Nations'.
12 UN. The World's Women 2015. The World's Women 2015 (un.org).
13 Traditional economies include the tribute or gift economy, and barter systems.
14 See Drèze and Sen (2013) *An Uncertain Glory: India and its Contradictions*. Princeton University Press pp. 58–64.
15 These were introduced in the 2010 Human Development Report titled 'The Real Wealth of Nations'.

16 Ruth Benedict (1946). *The Chrysanthemum and the Sword: Patterns of Japanese Culture.* Houghton Mifflin.
17 William Dubois (1903). *The Souls of Black Folk: Essays and Sketches.* A.C. McClurg & Co., Chicago.
18 See Nancy Fraser (2000). Rethinking Recognition, *New Left Review* 3, May–June 2000.
19 Narayan, Deepa et al. (2000). *Voices of the Poor: Crying Out for Change.* New York: Oxford University Press for the World Bank.

References

Benedict, Ruth. *The Chrysanthemum and the Sword: Patterns of Japanese Culture.* Boston: Houghton Mifflin (1946).
Drèze, Jean, and Amartya Sen. *An Uncertain Glory: India and Its Contradictions.* Princeton: Princeton University Press (2013).
Dubois, William. *The Souls of Black Folk: Essays and Sketches.* Chicago: A. C. McClurg & Co. (1903).
Fraser, Nancy. Rethinking Recognition. *New Left Review* 3(3):107–118 (2000).
Jackson, Tim. *Prosperity without Growth. Foundations for the Economy of Tomorrow.* London: Routledge (2009).
Narayan, Deepa, Chambers, Robert, Shah, Meera K., and Petesch, Patti. *Voices of the Poor: Crying Out for Change.* New York: Oxford University Press for the World Bank (2000).
Sachs, Jeffrey. *World Happiness Report* (2022). https://worldhappiness.rep ort/ed/2022/
Stewart, Frances. *Horizontal Inequalities and Conflict. Understanding Group Violence in Multiethnic Societies.* London: Palgrave Macmillan (2008).
Stiglitz, Joseph. *Globalization and Its Discontents.* New York/London: W.W. Norton & Company (2002).
Times of India. India's income inequality has doubled in 20 years. 7 December 2011. https://timesofindia.indiatimes.com/india/indias-income-inequality-has-doubled-in-20-years/articleshow/11012855.cms
UK Office for National Statistics. Initial investigation into subjective well-being from the Opinions Survey (2011).
UN Women. Facts and Figures: Economic Empowerment. UN Women – Headquarters. www.unwomen.org/en/what-we-do/economic-empowerm ent/facts-and-figures
United Nations. The Real Wealth of Nations. https://hdr.undp.org/content/ human-development-report-2010
United Nations. The Report of the High-Level Meeting on Wellbeing and Happiness Defining a New Economic Paradigm. New York: United Nations

Headquarters (2 April 2012). https://sustainabledevelopment.un.org/index.
php?page=view&type=400&nr=617&menu=35
United Nations. The World's Women (2015). https://unstats.un.org/unsd/gen
der/downloads/worldswomen2015_report.pdf
World Economic Forum. Women own less than 20% of the world's land. It's
time to give them equal property rights (2017). www.weforum.org/agenda/
2017/01/women-own-less-than-20-of-the-worlds-land-its-time-to-give-
them-equal-property-rights/

3 Research sites, women, and concepts involved in a study of the struggle for equality in rural India

Villages studied

The interviews take place in the Palni (Palani) Hills, Dindigul district. The town of Kodaikanal, Dindigul district is in a high basin about 2,150 metres above sea level. Dindigul district is the largest

Figure 3.1 Tamil Nadu map showing Dindigul district.

DOI: 10.4324/9781003519409-3

district in Tamil Nadu among 38 state districts. In 2006, Dindigul district was officially designated as one of India's 250 most backward districts.[1] It is one of the six districts in Tamil Nadu receiving funds from the Backward Regions Grant Fund Programme. Scheduled Castes accounted for 20.95% of the population of Dindigul district, and Scheduled Tribes just 0.37%.

The following five villages studied are in Dindigul district, which has 60 villages. For reasons of confidentiality, the village names are not identified. Instead, the villages are designated by the following codes: Dalit Village 1 (DV 1), Dalit Village 2 (DV 2), Adivasi Village 1 (AV 1), Adivasi Village 2 (AV 2) and Tamil Sri Lankan Repatriate Village (TSLRV).

Approach. Multidimensional wellbeing

The starting point is recognition that the wellbeing of rural marginalised women in the high country of Tamil Nadu is dependent on *access to opportunities*. In large part, this means job opportunities beyond rural casual work; but ultimately, it means equal opportunities to live the life that the women have reason to value.[2] In a state where women are close to gender parity in tertiary education achievements,[3] this implies that education is a necessary but insufficient indicator of wellbeing in the absence of empowerment. Accordingly, the formulation of variables and indicators in this study is based on interconnections between empowerment/decision-making and multiple dimensions of wellbeing capabilities.

As shown in Table 3.1, the dimensions of wellbeing are grouped under two headings: capabilities and equalities. 'Capabilities' comprise living standard/livelihoods, health and education, while 'equalities' are composed of self-efficacy, social action and human rights.

Table 3.1 Wellbeing dimensions

Wellbeing dimensions	
Capabilities	*Equalities*
Living standard/ livelihoods	Self-efficacy
Health	Social actions
Education	Human rights

Each dimension is equally weighted in the overall wellbeing index, as they are considered equally important for wellbeing.

Conceptual underpinnings. Theorising empowerment

The Beijing Declaration and Platform for Action is the well-established global plan for advancing women's rights.[4] It envisions a world where every woman and girl can exercise her freedoms and capabilities and enjoy her human rights. This includes living free from violence, engaging in decisions about one's own life, having access to similar healthcare and education experiences that men and boys have, and benefiting from opportunities to work on an equal footing with them. The Beijing Plan imagined gender equality in *all* dimensions of life for *all* women. It refuses over-simplification focused on a single dimension of equality – as attempted by the orthodoxy's 'Shared Prosperity' doctrine.[5]

The Beijing vision builds on a significant legacy including Mary Wollstonecraft's late 18th century work titled *A Vindication of the Rights of Woman*.[6] While Wollstonecraft insists that wellbeing and empowerment are inextricably joined in the struggle for equality, it

Table 3.2 Composite conceptualisation of empowerment education

Empowerment education is the development of multidimensional capabilities and social action strategies, beyond awareness-raising; It is literacy beyond a functional level, which enables a greater sense of agency but is just a precursor to transformation of power relations.
Sources: Stromquist, Nelly (2002). *Education in a Globalized World: The Connectivity of Economic Power, Technology, and Knowledge.* Rowman & Littlefield Publishers; and Prins, Esther (2016) Adult literacy education, gender equity and empowerment: Insights from a Freirean-inspired literacy programme. *Studies in the Education of Adults*, 40:1, 24-39

was not until the onset of the 21ˢᵗ century that researchers followed her lead. A prime example of capability research that does so is Amartya Sen's 1999 work *Development as Freedom*,[7] with its recognition that inequalities severely weaken wellbeing. Other work has advanced Wollstonecraft's recognition through focus on empowerment or self-help. Typically, this centres on adult education in public spaces where people debate their conditions, examine them and seek mutualising solutions. Gramsci is an important figure in this work. In the second decade of the 1900s, he advocated adult/social learning through factory councils in order to enable self-help through increased awareness of unequal power relations.[8] In subsequent work, the American feminist movement has carried out empowerment approaches since the mid-1960s.

In the latter part of the 20ᵗʰ century, Jürgen Habermas also promoted similar social education approaches,[9] while in the global south, in particular, Paulo Freire's *Pedagogy of the Oppressed* advanced understanding of the intersections of empowerment and adult/social education. Typically, this is in the framework of liberation theology.[10] His work transfers recognition that agent-oriented learning approaches focused on power relations help oppressed people to regain their humanity in the struggle for empowerment.[11]

The Grihini programme which partners the development of this book takes a Freirean approach to adult/social education. Its work is characterised by the liberatory content of classes that centre on learners' lived experiences. Historically, the college was established as a non-formal education centre in 1987. The programme was designed for deprived/vulnerable women living in rural districts of Tamil Nadu. Grihini has since provided education for over 2,000 women from the poorest groups who live and work in the Palni Hills. 34 years after its inception, Grihini became an accredited Community College, providing certificated skills programmes and academic coaching programmes to assist young women to pass the government year 10 and 12 exams in addition to literacy and social awareness programmes.[12]

The focus of Grihini is on skills in cultural as well as functional literacy, developed through solving problems that women face in their villages. The notion of 'cultural literacy' in Freirean terms signifies critical reflection and acting on awareness of 'how people labor, create, and make life choices'.[13] Accordingly, the purpose of Freirean approaches to cultural literacy accentuates the necessity of choice-making, in order to resist injustice and wrest power away from oppressive social, economic, political and cultural conditions.[14]

Notes

1 *Backward areas* means socially, economically, educationally and industrially under-developed areas, and usually pertains to hilly, drought-prone and backward areas as so declared by the appropriate government.
2 This is the definition of the capabilities approach widely articulated by Sen and Nussbaum.
3 Tamil Nadu has 50.5% male enrolment and 49.5% female enrolment in higher education, according to The All India Survey of Higher Education (AISHE) 2019. TN sees more gender parity in higher education but there's plenty of scope for improvement – *The New Indian Express*.
4 UN Women. The Beijing Platform for Action Turns 20.
5 See Shane Chalmers & Pahuja, op. cit.
6 Mary Wollstonecraft (1792) *A Vindication of the Rights of Woman*. The text is in the public domain.
7 Sen, A. (1999) *Development as Freedom. Ch 8. Women's Agency and Social Change*. (1st ed.). New York: Oxford University Press,
8 Mayo, Peter (2014) Antonio Gramsci's Impact on Critical Pedagogy, *Critical Sociology*, February 7, 2014.
9 Habermas, J (1987). *The Theory of Communicative Action*. Vol. II: *Lifeworld and System*, T. McCarthy (trans.). Boston: Beacon.
10 Freire, P. (2005). *Pedagogy of the Oppressed*. Transl. Myra Bergman Ramos. New York: Continuum.
11 E.g., Cervero, R., & Wilson, A. L. (Eds.). (2001). Power in practice. San Francisco: Jossey-Bass.
Nesbit, T., & Wilson, A.L. (2003). Theorizing power. Proceedings of the 44th annual adult education research conference (pp. 309–314). San Francisco: San Francisco State University.
Wilson, A. L., & Nesbit, T. (2005). The Problem of Power. Proceedings of the 46th Annual Adult Education Research Conference (unpaginated). San Francisco: San Francisco State University.
12 See Jan Orrell, An Amma Story 'More than being able to read'. Grihini – Stories | Norman Habel. Also, on the liberatory characterisation of Freirean approaches, see the works of Shor & Freire, 1987; and Facundo, 1984.
13 Wallerstein, 1983, p. 5.
14 Jurmo (1987).

References

All India Survey of Higher Education (AISHE). 'TN Sees More Gender Parity in Higher Education but There's Plenty of Scope for Improvement'. *New Indian Express* (2019).
Cervero, Ronald M., & Wilson, Arthur L. (Eds.). *Power in Practice*. San Francisco: Jossey-Bass (2001).

34   *Research sites, women, and concepts*

Chalmers, Shane, and Sundhya Pahuja. 'The Inequity of Development: Reading the World Bank's Turn to Inequality'. In Antony Anghie, Bhupinder Chimni, Michael Fakhri, Karin Mickelson and Vasuki Nesiah (eds.), *Handbook of Third World Approaches to International Law*. Edward Elgar (forthcoming).

Facundo, Blanca. *Freire Inspired Programs in the United States and Puerto Rico: A Critical Evaluation*. Washington, D.C.: The Latino Institute (1984). www.dropbox.com/scl/fi/444yed8fx6n8v1hqr57xt/Blanca-Facundo. pdf?rlkey=geylbe6lqt516o6nvsgarbwhx&e=1

Freire, Paulo. *Pedagogy of the Oppressed*. Transl. Myra Bergman Ramos. New York: Continuum (2005).

Habermas, Jürgen. *The Theory of Communicative Action. Vol. II: Lifeworld and System*. Thomas McCarthy (trans.). Boston: Beacon (1987).

Jurmo, Paul Joseph. Learner Participation Practices in Adult Literacy Efforts in the United States. *Doctoral Dissertations 1896 – February 2014*. 2030 (1987). https://scholarworks.umass.edu/dissertations_1/2030

Mayo, Peter. Antonio Gramsci's Impact on Critical Pedagogy. *Critical Sociology* 41(7–8), 1121–1136 (2014).

Nesbit, Tom, and Wilson, Arthur L. 'Theorizing Power'. *Proceedings of the 44th Annual Adult Education Research Conference* (pp. 309–314). San Francisco: San Francisco State University (2003).

Orrell, Jan. An Amma Story 'More than being able to read'. In Janice Orrell (ed.), *Grihini: Stories of Hope and Liberation*, p. 37. Adelaide: Norman Habel.

Ramakrishnan, Sushmitha; New India Express. TN sees more gender parity in higher education but there's plenty of scope for improvement. Updated on: 20 June 2021. www.newindianexpress.com/states/tamil-nadu/2021/Jun/19/tn-sees-more-gender-parity-in-higher-education-but-theres-plenty-of-scope-for-improvement-2318676.html

Sen, Amartya. *Development as Freedom*. New York: Alfred Knopf (1999).

Shore, Ira, and Freire, Paolo. What is the 'dialogical method' of teaching? *Journal of Education*, 169(3), 11–31 (1987).

UN Women. The Beijing Declaration and Platform for Action Turns 20. (2015). https://sustainabledevelopment.un.org/content/documents/1776 The%20Beijing%20Declaration%20and%20Platform%20for%20Action%20turns%2020.pdf

Wallerstein, Nina. *Language and Culture in Conflict: Problem-Posing in the ESL Classroom*. Reading, MA: Addison-Wesley (1983).

Wilson, Arthur, and Nesbit, Tom. 'The Problem of Power'. *Proceedings of the 46th Annual Adult Education Research Conference* (unpaginated). San Francisco: San Francisco State University (2005).

Wollstonecraft, Mary. *A Vindication of the Rights of Woman with Strictures on Political and Moral Subjects*. London: J. Johnson (1792).

4   Research processes involved in a wellbeing inquiry of rural women's struggle for equality in India

The measurement tool

The measurement system in this study draws on and adapts Bhutan's Gross National Happiness (GNH) initiative, and consequently on the work of the Oxford Poverty and Human Development Initiative (OPHI) led by Sabina Alkire. As previously noted, these methods contrast markedly with orthodox calculations which insist that income (gross national income / gross domestic product) is the measure of *progress*. The difference is that the GNH/OPHI system is multidimensional and allots equal value to both non-economic and economic aspects of 'progress'. As discussed elsewhere in the book, this draws on an array of indicators which both uncover power relationships that thwart access to opportunities, as well as identify opportunities that need opening up in living standards, health and education.

The quantification of rural women's wellbeing in this study is based on interviews at individual, household and village levels. The idea is to capture subjective and objective variables across two dimensions of wellbeing – capabilities and equalities – as already noted. Table 4.1 shows the composition of the measurement system with its 23 indicators of capabilities and 22 indicators of equalities.

The Alkire–Foster methodology[1] is the basis of the indices measurement. In this index system, the step of identifying who falls into the category of 'maintained wellbeing' or 'not maintained wellbeing' relies on two cut-offs. One is within each domain to determine the category (maintained or not maintained) with respect to each variable in that domain. The second cut-off is a nominal one that is applied across domains. This nominal cut-off identifies individuals who are in the category ('maintained' or 'not maintained') sufficiency in wellbeing.

DOI: 10.4324/9781003519409-4

Table 4.1 Indicators of wellbeing

Capabilities		Equalities	
Living standard/ livelihood	1. Engaged in paid work?	**Self-efficacy**	1. Level of self-esteem
	2. COVID-19 impact on paid work?		2. Level of confidence to participate in decision-making, employability communications, handling problems & facing challenges
	3. Income sufficiency?		3. Interest in women's political & social status
	4. Own scooter or motorbike?		4. Active engagement in empowerment courses/ programmes
	5. Access to nearby buses?		5. Benefits from empowerment courses in relation to confidence, work, & education
	6. Access to electricity supply?		6. Active engagement with women's concerns
	7. Access to a toilet?		7. Active engagement with environmental concerns
	8. Access to drinking water?		8. Level of concern for environmental crises
	9. Indebtedness?		9. Participation in decisions about use of earnings
Health	10. Overall physical health	**Social action**	10. Participation in decisions about going to the market & places outside the village
	11. Current physical health		11. Participation in decisions about own healthcare
	12. Historical physical health		12. Participation in decisions about large household buys
	13. Mental health status in past year		13. Participation in decisions about own education
	14. COVID-19 impact on physical & mental health		14. Opinion on right to make work/job decisions
	15. Prevalence of anxiety or depression		15. Interest in political processes, including elections
	16. Access to nearby health facility		
	17. Enough income for food, shelter, medicines		

Education

18. Food security (missing meals)
19. Literacy levels in Tamil & English
20. Education achievement level
21. Constraints on education access
22. Skills in managing money, computers, smartphone, & public speaking/job interviews (indicator of empowerment also)
23. Access to internet

Human rights

16. Freedom to speak freely about political & government issues.
17. Opinion on equal opportunity & access to work
18. Awareness of availability of state welfare benefits
19. Experience & prevalence of household violence
20. Is a man justified in hitting or beating women in the household (in various scenarios)?
21. Household head opinion on importance of education for women relative to marriage
22. Household head opinion on woman's right to make education decisions

This nominal cut-off is calculated by counting the domains in which a person has achieved sufficiency in maintaining wellbeing.

To measure wellbeing in each domain, a 'two-thirds rule' is applied for calculations at each of the domains. For example, there are three variables in the capabilities domain. This means that the maximum score an individual could obtain in this domain is 3 (that is, if the participant scores 1 in each variable). The minimum score is 0 (that is, if the participant scores 0 in each variable), where the scores 1 and 0 denote achievement or non-achievement of sufficiency in a variable. By the two-thirds rule, an individual (the participant) would need to score a minimum of 6 to be considered as having achieved sufficiency in maintaining wellbeing in this domain. The domain is then recoded as 0 for those who scored less than 6, and 1 for those who scored 6 or more. Thus, the number of respondents would be distributed between a score of 0 and a score of 1. In this way, each domain has a distribution of respondents with a score of either 0 or 1.

The level of overall wellbeing achievement of an individual (for all domains combined) is obtained by adding up the domain scores. These calculations are referred to in this book as the composite Capabilities Index and Equalities Index, respectively. The two-thirds rule is applied again here to determine whether the individual has maintained overall wellbeing or not. An individual is defined as 'maintained overall wellbeing' if that individual scored 1 each in at least any four domains out of the total of six domains.

Profile of interviewees

Interview procedure

Based on prior consent and full disclosure[2] a set of two different structured questionnaires was administered in five villages to 150 individual women and 150 of the women's household representatives. Two of the villages are predominantly Dalit, two are Tribal villages and one is home to Sri Lankan Tamil Repatriates (ex-bonded labourers). About half the women interviewees and their household representatives have experience of social/adult education delivered by the Grihini programme, and about half do not.

Subsequently, focus group discussions (FGDs) took place with a village representative/leader in each of the five villages. FGD participants included two women. The FGD aim was to investigate

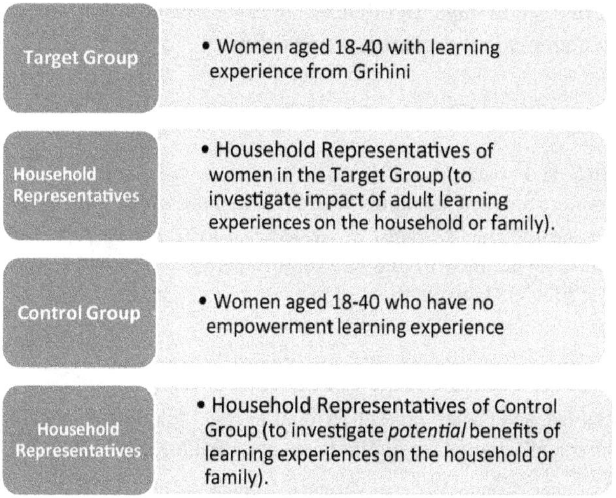

Figure 4.1 Profile of interviewees.

the social or community values or perceived benefits/disadvantages of women's empowerment education.

The content of survey and FGD questions is the result of collaboration with the Grihini programme team who, in turn, identify the survey sites, recruit and manage a team of non-Grihini-College-affiliated field workers, carry out the data entry and collaborated on analysis and writing of this book.

The choice of using convenience sampling is shaped by mitigation policies for the COVID-19 crisis. In addition to direct damage done by the coronavirus, the resulting lockdowns seriously ravaged healthcare-deprived highland populations (see 'Contexts and Analysis of Survey of Individual Women' in Chapter Five). *Convenience sampling* recruits interviewees who are available in a location (village) as sources of research data. Women's network leaders in the region identified availability and assisted the consent and recruitment process by letting villagers know that they sought expressions of interest/consent to engage in interviews. The process ensures confidentiality and familiarity with the aims of the research and the rights of consultants. Following consent, the research fieldwork team travelled by cars to the location/villages of participants. Some villages are sufficiently large that the interviewers could schedule and complete the interviews over a period of several days. In other villages the availability numbers are lower, which made the interview rates slower.

Notes

1 Alkire S. and Foster J.E. (2011)
2 The project proposal complied with the principles of the *Australian Code for the Responsible Conduct of Research (2018)* and its supplementary guidance, as certified by the Research Integrity, Ethics and Compliance team at Flinders University.

Reference

Alkire, Sabina, and Foster, James E. 'Counting and Multidimensional Poverty Measurement'. *Journal of Public Economics*, 95(7–8), 476–487 (2011).

5 Outcomes of a quality-of-life study of marginalised women's struggle for equality in India

Contexts and analysis of survey of individual women

The analysis of individual women participants compares data collected from women who are poor and marginalised, among whom some have experience of Grihini adult/social education and others have no experience of adult/social education workshops or classes. It helps understanding of the findings to consider how Grihini graduates have no power advantage or entitlement over others. On the contrary, the findings show that Grihini graduates and their household representatives have lower health status, less education, fewer jobs and more hardship from COVID interventions. The more important point is that all rural marginalised women in the region invariably belong to the most deprived/vulnerable social groupings as a result of social class and race-based discrimination. Readers will notice that this circumstance shapes the form of the following analysis which is often based on the entire sample population ('all women'). This rationale also influences the composition of the indices.

At the same time, readers can anticipate significant benefits connected with adult/social education. These benefits show up in responses from both Grihini respondents and their household representatives. Prime examples of empowerment include confidence, decision-making, navigating life's challenges, and skills that help an individual express herself and engage with others. Moreover, Grihini graduates are much more likely to engage in decision-making regarding their health, household purchases and going alone to places outside the home. Further details are discussed below.

Another context that matters when considering the findings is that while the respondents are vulnerable/deprived, they are not just

DOI: 10.4324/9781003519409-5

victims; they are also people who deliberate about what they should do and act on the basis of such pondering, and they resolve through consideration the questions about what one is to do, based on what one values. This characterises the possession of 'practical reason' as well as 'capability', as articulated by Amartya Sen, a founding figure of human development approaches.[1] Examples of 'practical reason' in this book include the women's recognition of environmental threats caused by the climate crisis. This is aptly called practical reason because among the multiple specialisations that rural women take up, they are agriculturists with custodianship of sustainable food gardens. Another context that is considered critical for interpreting the findings is the impact of lockdowns related to COVID-19. In the broad context of rural India, the most significant COVID-19 containment measure was the national lockdown on 22 March 2020, which led to extensions until 31 May 2020.[2] These mitigation measures produced severe unemployment and loss of income in rural Indian households. As a result, households consumed less food and in some instances turned to loans to meet expenses. Access to healthcare was a particular issue for rural households. A 2021 study by Rohan et al. shows that about one-quarter of 607 households studied in rural Tamil Nadu had family members who required monthly medications for chronic medical conditions such as hypertension and/or diabetes.[3]

66 *Has COVID-19 caused you to experience physical or mental health problems?' 45% of women respondents in this study said 'Yes'.*
Cross-checking question: 'Have you suffered from anxiety or depression in the past 12 months?' 58% of respondents said 'Yes'.

Emergency medical assistance during the lockdown was problematic due to lack of transport, inability to leave the house because of the lockdown, and closure of health centres. Lack of public transportation was a recurring issue for rural households in Tamil Nadu, together with inflated private transport fares.

Most households in rural Tamil Nadu receive government ration supplies. Most found this insufficient during the lockdowns, given a loss of income through unemployment. Some households received supplies from nongovernmental organisations (NGOs) operating in the area. This includes support by the Grihini programme for some families in the location of this book's research.

Schools in Tamil Nadu were closed on 16 March 2020. The government provided laptop computers to children in the 11th grade or higher. For those children in lower grades, this meant using smartphones to connect to online classes. It was a very limited option that applied to device owners. But even then, poor network connectivity affected attendance at online classes. Furthermore, female children in rural Tamil Nadu were kept busy with household chores during online classes – because they were there at home.[4]

> 66 *Has COVID-19 meant you lost your job / daily wage / study opportunities?' 68% of all respondents in this study said 'Yes'.*
>
> *Cross-checking question: 'Have you done any work other than your housework in the past 12 months?' One-third of all women respondents said 'Yes'.*

About 32% of households took out loans during the lockdown.[5] Most found it difficult to repay the loans. Procuring vegetables/provisions and potable water and paying electricity bills and school fees became challenging. Daily-wage workers were the most affected by a decline in weekly wages during the lockdowns. They lost their jobs. The workers most likely to become unemployed during the lockdowns were from low-income households. They had significantly greater odds of being unemployed during the lockdown, along with individuals with no savings.[6]

> *Women respondents in this Dindigul study said that in almost one-quarter of the time in the past year they ate less because there wasn't enough food or money.*

Farmers could not take their produce to markets because they were closed. Farming inputs (seeds, fertilisers, pesticides) were out of reach for vulnerable households due to inflated prices. Non-deferment of previous loans worsened the predicament for households in debt. In

Table 5.1 Taxonomy of response analysis

Capabilities	Equalities
Living standards/livelihoods	Self-efficacy
Health	Social actions
Education	Human rights

the absence of targeted public policy interventions, the lockdowns exacerbated already-stretched access to livelihoods for many rural marginalised people – thus undermining wellbeing through blocked access to healthcare, as a single example.

The analysis of responses from 150 individual women is based on the following taxonomy:

To facilitate reading, the contraction *GR* is used for 'Grihini respondents'; and *non-GR* is used for 'non-Grihini respondents'.

Living standard/livelihoods

- Regarding ownership of a computer or smartphone, the data show that GR (43%) are relatively deprived in terms of living standards when this question is compared with non-GR (49%).
- GR are more likely to own a bicycle, which can be taken as a sign of relative deprivation in terms of living standards, particularly in the context of the data showing that non-GR are more likely to own a motor scooter or motorbike.
- More than 60% of all women respondents had jobs in addition to housework in the past 12 months (a period that importantly overlaps with the COVID-19 crisis). GR are less likely to have done such work compared to non-GR. This confirms a point included in the contextual section above regarding the relative deprivation of Grihini women regarding living standards.
- GR who did work at jobs in addition to housework and were paid in cash or in kind (61%) were much less likely to have been paid than non-GR (70%). A possible implication, based on other data on self-efficacy, is that this could be related to a heightened sense of mutuality in a time of pandemic.
- COVID-19 mitigation lockdowns were intensely felt by rural highland villages in various ways that include job and earnings losses,

as noted. This survey shows that 68% of all women respondents reported losing their job / daily wage / study opportunities.

• Importantly, in terms of cross-generational debt, 38% of all women respondents have (ever) taken out a bank loan or used a credit card. Slightly fewer GR compared with non-GR have ever taken out loans or used a credit card. Significantly more GR than non-GR who took out a bank loan used it to set up an enterprise, rather than using it for other purposes such as house repairs or daily expenses or a vehicle purchase.

• Most of all women respondents *have* taken a loan from a non-bank lender. Most frequently this was from one of two sources: a co-worker or an employer. Importantly for intergenerational indebtedness, 58% of women who have taken such a loan *were* able to repay it in full. Conversely, this means that a disconcerting number (42%) have *not* been able to repay it in full. This situation leads to accumulative generational debt.

• While additional data show that GR are relatively more deprived money-wise than non-GR, all respondents endure a shared condition of financial hardship. 45% of all respondents stated that their current income was insufficient to pay for food, shelter, medicines and education. This finding is alarming on multiple levels. For one, it is a key driver of the lack of wellbeing (see Chapter Six 'Wellbeing indices'). On a second level that pertains to health, the World Health Organization (WHO) calls such situations *catastrophic* where there are insufficient funds to pay for medicine. Health expenditure is called *catastrophic* whenever the measure of the burden of health care expenditure (out-of-pocket costs) is greater than or equal to 40% of the capacity of a household's available resources to pay.[7]

> *Women respondents as a grouping said that just under one-quarter of the time in the past year they ate less because there wasn't enough food or money.*

• All women respondents as a grouping said that just under one-quarter of the time in the past year they ate less because there was not enough food or money. This is an acute result of the impact of COVID-19 that impacts on all of the multiple dimensions of wellbeing – and in this research ultimately adversely affects the Wellbeing Index.

Education/literacy

> *18% of all women respondents have never completed any education.*

- The highest level of education completed by all women respondents (37%) was up to tenth standard (which equates to an age of around 16 years). 14% of all respondents stated that their highest level completed was secondary school, while 5% and 7% completed Certificate and Diploma levels, respectively. While these data are encouraging – even in a state that has done well in education – there are worrying education data that persist. Worst is the finding that 18% of all women respondents have never completed any education. 25% of the responses to this question were from non-GR, whereas 13% were from GR.
- An important Tamil Nadu context to reiterate is the literacy gap of rural women. According to the most recent (2011) India Census, female rural literacy lagged at 65%, behind rural male literacy which stood at 82%.[8]
- On the question of specific factors that *prevent* respondents from gaining an education, 61% of all respondents answered 'Yes' to finance. Slightly less than 50% of all women respondents said 'family permission' was a specific barrier, and 43% stated that 'access to transportation' was a reason. Noticeably, GR (46%) were more likely to see transport as a problem compared with non-GR (40%). Again, this points to the relative deprivation/vulnerability of GR in terms of inadequate access to transportation to pursue education.

Health

> *51% of all women respondents self-reported mental health issues 'in the past 12 months' (coinciding with COVID-19 lockdowns)*

- Adverse health impacts from COVID-19 mitigation measures are reported by 45% of all women respondents. Noticeably, GR (40%) suffered less in this respect than non-GR (52%).

- 51% of all women respondents self-reported mental health issues in the period of 'the past 12 months' (the time frame of COVID lockdowns). As a side note, the finding that lockdowns led to worse mental health outcomes shows up in other studies that include research from the Australian National University (ANU) based on the Oxford University Stringency Index.[9] The ANU study corroborates findings by Saikia et al. that are based on a wellbeing measurement system.[10]
- The result that 19% of all women respondents self-report ill-health that lasted over six months again underscores the significance of the *catastrophic* characterisation used by the WHO to describe the impact caused by a lack of adequate means for healthcare.
- An additional health question in the survey asks *'How satisfied were you with your physical ability to do everyday activities, in the past week?'* A disturbingly large percentage of all women respondents (19%) were *dissatisfied*.
- The survey includes a baseline health question that asks *'On the whole, how would you rate your physical health?'*.[11] 13% of GR answered *'not good'*, compared with 3% of non-GR. This finding that especially affects Grihini women correlates with previously noted findings on their relatively higher income poverty. GR (47%) show they are more deprived financially than non-GR (41%) in responses indicating whether their current income was sufficient to pay for food, shelter, medicines and education. Previously mentioned additional data that point to the correlation of health and income deprivations include the finding that 8% of GR ate less in the past year because there wasn't enough food or money, compared to 10% of non-GR. As shown later in the Wellbeing Index, this factor drives the lack of wellbeing.

Self-efficacy

> 58% of Grihini graduate women self-report 'excellent' capability in public speaking.

Confidence in communicating/public speaking is one of the key benefits that shows up among the positive impacts of adult/social education. Respondents were asked 'How capable are you in public speaking (convincing other people)?'. 58% of GR self-reported '*excellent*' capability, compared to 48% of non-GR. A cross-checking question was asked on the women's 'level of confidence in communicating confidently'. The proportion of '*excellent*' responses among GR (48%) was higher compared with non-GR (32%).

> *65% of all women said they participate in decisions about how their earnings will be used.*

- An additional strong indication of self-efficacy pertaining to *all* women respondents is the finding that only 4% of respondents reported a *poor* 'level of confidence in handling problems and facing challenges'.
- In the struggle for equality, a further consequential finding is that 64.7% of all women said they participate in decisions about how their earnings will be used. Responses to a similar question found that 40% of GR 'make *most* of the household decisions about education', compared with 30% of non-GR. Furthermore, the responses to a further question involving participation in decisions about the women's own healthcare uncover an important result: only 7% of all respondents said 'No' – they do not participate.

A separate study to the one in this book that corroborates findings of women's participation in decision-making involves women in rural West Bengal.[12] That study found that 'education was effective' in transforming participation in farming decisions. The authors found greater frequencies of effectiveness among 'forward castes', but the study also found 'progress' by Adivasi and Dalit women in joint decision-making by both female and male participants.

Human rights

> *69% of all women respondents stated that a man is NOT justified in hitting or beating a woman in the household if she argues with him.*

• A potent indicator of human rights in this study concerns questions about violence in the family. The distressing nature of this theme suggests it is useful to initially emphasise progressive findings. There are healthy percentages of women respondents who refuse to accept violence in the various settings that the survey posed: 67% of all women respondents stated that 'a man is NOT justified in hitting or beating a woman in the household if she goes out without telling him'. In response to a follow-up question of 'whether a man is justified in hitting or beating the women if they argue with him', 69% of all women respondents again said 'No'.

The same number of all women respondents answered 'No' to the question that asks whether violence is justified if 'they don't cook the food properly'. However, fewer women (59%) said 'No' to a follow-up question on the hypothetical 'If he suspects his wife of having an extramarital affair'. Explanations of these findings where many women continue to accept violence imply the persistence of enculturation/patriarchy. On the other hand, inferred progress in the struggle for equality plays a demonstrable part in trying to explain why a significant percentage of these women now say 'No'.

Yet it remains that human rights violations (violence) are severe for high numbers of women respondents. 44% of all women respondents reported that they 'suffer emotionally or physically from violence in the family'. In 15% of these cases, violence occurs 'very often'. When these data are cross-tabulated with findings on self-reported mental health issues in the past 12 months, 51% of all women respondents say they experienced mental health issues. Note that the latter data represent the time frame of COVID-19.

Social actions

• As a background note, this book transfers an assumption that self-reported confidence does not necessarily reflect social action, nor equality in the final instance. More specifically, actions/ achievements are viewed as the glue in the joining-up of wellbeing and empowerment – and thus go well beyond increased feelings of self-worth.

> *Almost one-third of Grihini graduates reported that they had attended a village or town meeting or discussion on gender inequality and/or environmental concerns in the past 12 months.*

- On the issue of correlation between self-worth and social action, the survey asks respondents whether they 'attended a village or town meeting or discussion on gender inequality and/or environmental concerns in the past 12 months'. Almost one-third of GR (32%) report they had done so. Significantly, so too had a similar percentage of non-GR.

> *Grihini adult education graduates (35%) are much more likely to go alone outside the village **most of the time** compared with non-GR participants (24%)*

- A forceful indicator of the positive impacts of adult/social education towards equality is the finding that GR (35%) are *much* more likely to go alone outside the village 'most of the time' compared with non-GR (24%). GR (35%) are also much more likely to go alone to the health facility 'most of the time', compared with non-GR (25%). In addition, GR (30%) are also significantly more likely to go alone to the market 'most of the time', compared with non-GR (24%).

  On the other hand, among *all* women respondents, 61% 'rarely do so'. The contexts that matter very much here are religious and social, whereby social isolation of women is mandated for many.

- Finally in this section, interviewees are asked five cross-checking questions on the theme of 'level of concern for deforestation, water pollution, air pollution, land pollution/waste, and extinction of wildlife'. The percentage of all women respondents who expressed 'deep concern' for these issues ranges between 72 and 75%.

> *The percentage of all women respondents who expressed 'deep concern' for environmental issues ranged between 72 and 75%.*

This is a consequential finding. It seemingly reflects the fact that the prevalent livelihoods of women respondents are farm-focused. In other words, their enlightened responses as agronomists could be expected. 'Enlightened responses' suggests heritage traditions of land custodianship and customary practices that are long held. On the other hand, climate change renders such traditions outdated in many cases. Environmental conditions are uncertain due to impacts of the climate crisis. This means that environmental education plays a crucial role in the renewal of 'enlightened' rural practices. Fittingly, the adult/social education curriculum of Grihini explicitly tackles the acute issue of climate.

Analysis of survey of household representatives

As noted, 150 household representatives of the women who participate in the individual survey were interviewed. 'Household representatives' denotes individuals who elect to represent the households of participants in the survey of individual women. The following analysis is based on similar dimensions of capabilities and equalities that were used in the women's survey analysis. However, there is a difference in the analyses due to the different *content* of the questionnaires. The individual women's survey probes the issues of subjective wellbeing (and empowerment), whereas the household representatives' survey investigates the *social* impacts of women's pursuit of wellbeing (and empowerment) while additionally uncovering the manifold social–economic circumstances of women's struggles for wellbeing/equality.

To facilitate focus on the following findings, the analysis of the household representative survey folds the three streams of equalities (self-efficacy, human rights and social actions) into a single stream of 'equalities'. There is a second point of analytic difference between the women's and the household representatives' surveys: the analysis of the women's survey has focused on 'all women respondents' as a gender grouping as a means to shed light on the sampled women's wellbeing (capabilities + equalities), whereas the analysis of the household representatives' survey fits a different purpose by differentiating/comparing the responses of Grihini-engaging household representatives and non-Grihini-engaging household representatives. To facilitate reading, the contraction GHR is used for 'Grihini-engaging household representatives', and non-GHR is used for 'non-Grihini-engaging household representatives'.

The following points characterise the profile of the household representatives:

*   58% of all household representatives have member(s) of their household who have engaged with Grihini adult/social education; and 42% do not.
*   97.3% of the respondents are male.
*   33% of GHR self-identify as Adivasi compared with 51% in the case of non-GHR. 26% of GHR self-identify as Dalit compared with 24% in the case of non-GHR. 17% of GHR self-identify as Sri Lankan Tamil compared with 14% in the case of non-GHR.
*   18% of all household head respondents self-identified as 'none of the above'. They are neither Tribal nor Scheduled Caste, but they are lowered caste who are officially designated as 'backward' and 'most backward', and economically poor.
*   On the count of people currently residing in these households, 56% number between four and five people in the case of GHR, compared with 54% of non-GHR in this same number range.
*   80% of respondents have lived in the village/town all their life. GHR (76%) are less likely to have lived all their life in the village/town than non-GHR (86%).
*   63% of GHR work as plantation labourers, compared with 73% in the case of non-GHR. 23% of GHR are migrant workers, compared with 16% in the case of non-GHR. Migrant workers in the area of study are commonly involved in the cultivation and harvesting of garlic and vegetables (mainly potatoes, carrots and beans).

Capabilities findings

*   95% of the households do not own a bicycle; and 66% of all households do not own a motor scooter or motorbike. These statistics are significant when considering rural women's access to education and healthcare services, and the pursuit of work

opportunities and human rights entitlements through visits to public officials.

- 91% of households have electricity supply, while 9% do not have electricity supply.
- 79% of households have television. Of those who do not have television, significantly more are GHR (23%) than non-GHR (18%).
- 60% of households have a computer or smartphone. Of those who do not, significantly more are non-GHR (46%) than GHR (36%).
- 95% of all households do not have internet connection. The statistical difference between respondents reads non-GHR (97%) and GHR (94%).
- 97% of 'all the households' have a nearby bus connection, although the frequency of bus service is very limited and irregular. The key point is that transportation is a major factor in the lack of access to education. Importantly, and not captured by the data point of 'nearby bus connection' is that access to public transport is essentially a matter of affordability. It could cost more than a daily wage to get into Kodaikanal from the villages. Commuting to schools located in Kodaikanal every day is not possible. It could cost more than a daily wage to get into Kodaikanal from the villages.
- Almost all households (99%) do have drinking water supplied. This supports a component of the research of Sustainable Development Goals (SDGs) that Tamil Nadu has performed exceptionally well compared to all Indian states (tied in third place with Himachal Pradesh) on the SDGs dashboard.[13]

---

*39% of all households report that their total household income is **NOT** enough to pay for food, shelter, healthcare and education for all the members in their household.*

- Countering the positive impact of clean drinking water on sanitation improvements is the finding that 29.3% of all households have zero access to a toilet – let alone exclusive access to a toilet. Regarding exclusive access, just under half (54.7%) reported 'Yes'.
- A crucial living standard/livelihood question asks 'Is your total household income enough to pay for food, shelter, healthcare and education for all the members in your household?'. 39% of all households report that their total household income is insufficient

in this vital respect. GHR (44%) are significantly more deprived compared with non-GHR (32%).

- On this same question, 45% of all households **'sometimes'** 'have adequate total household income for food, shelter, healthcare and education'.
- This finding of **occasional insufficient** resources reflects, partially at least, the factor of a 'hunger season'. This refers to a particularly challenging time in the gardening cycle for subsistence farmers and their families, who rely solely on what they grow (typically for others' principal benefit). The 'hunger season' is the time of year between planting and harvest when food runs out. It can last for months. Also known as the 'lean season', this brings with it extreme (*catastrophic*) deprivation. Noteworthy for public policy and research communities is that this observation again acutely moderates the SDGs research conclusion that Tamil Nadu has done very well on the SDGs dashboard.
- A survey question investigating the impacts of COVID-19 on well-being found that 71% of households 'have at least one member who lost their job or income opportunities' [due to COVID mitigation]. This finding corroborates the women's survey data on the same question.

Against a backdrop of COVID-19, 43% of all households ate less in the past year because there wasn't enough food or money. For 12% of these households, this was 'most of the time'.

23% of all households reported that COVID-19 affected their family's physical or mental health.

- Again, in the context of COVID-19 impacts, 43% of all households 'ate less in the past year because there wasn't enough food or money'. For 12% of these households, this was 'most of the time'.
- More GHR (48%) ate less during this period because there wasn't enough food or money compared to non-GHR (33%). This further points to the relative living standard deprivations felt by Grihini-participating households, which concerns the observation that Grihini participants belong to a highly vulnerable population even within exceedingly deprived villages.

- Note that while the above finding is grouped under 'health', it has clear implications for livelihoods and ultimately illustrates the multidimensionality of wellbeing taken in this approach.
- An overarching health question in the survey asks 'Overall, how would you rate your family's physical health?'. While one-half of all households (50%) self-reported 'average' physical health, the statistics were significantly less for GHR (45%) compared with non-GHR (52%).
- The health vulnerability of household members becomes even more concerning when viewed alongside previously discussed adverse findings on: 1) insufficient total household income to pay for food, shelter, healthcare and education; and 2) frequency in the past year that member(s) of the household ate less because there wasn't enough food or money.
- In the area of mental or emotional health, one-third of respondents reported anxiety or depression in the past 12 months. Less than half (47%) of all respondents self-reported 'no suffering' in this regard. Again, for the public policy and research community, this damaging finding coincides with COVID mitigation measures.
- Further to COVID-19 experiences, 23% of all households report that COVID-19 affected their family's physical or mental health. Regarding the relative severity of this, significantly fewer GHR were affected in terms of physical or mental health: 51% of GHR reported 'not much' suffering health-wise compared with 37% of non-GHR.
- Turning to findings on a question that directly tackles the earlier-mentioned issue of catastrophic healthcare – 'Do you experience financial difficulties that prevent household members from health-related attention?' – 74% of all households said 'Yes'. GHR (77%) were considerably more likely than non-GHR (70%) to experience financial difficulties that prevent household members from seeking healthcare.
- On a question that asks about the household's *access* to healthcare, 12% of all households reported they do not have 'nearby' access to health centres or hospitals.

Equalities analysis

- Given that most household respondents are male (97%), a significant finding involves the question 'Who should have the greater say in decisions about how many children to have?'; 93% of all household representatives responded 'both husband and wife'.

• This response raises a query concerning the social influence of women's adult/social education. The uncertainty is that on the one hand, GHR (5%) are more likely than non-GHR (3%) to say a wife should have a greater say in this decision. On the other hand, the same percentage of GHR (5%) say a husband should have a greater say compared with just 2% of non-GR households. This ostensibly reflects the persistence of patriarchy in decision-making related to fertility (and reproductive health).

• Turning to a different set of questions, respondents with household member(s) who had done a course or workshop with a college, community-based organisation, or NGO were asked the following seven questions:

  • *Have the household member(s) learned skills to start and run their own business?* 69% of all households said 'Yes'. GHR (72%) were much more likely to say 'Yes' than non-GHR (64%).

  • *Have the women become more independent & self-reliant?* 81% of GHR said 'Yes', while considerably fewer non-GHR (68%) replied 'Yes'.

  • *Has it enabled your family members to secure a livelihood they had never had before?* 70% of GHR said 'Yes' compared with 54% of non-GHR.

  • *Has it raised your family's self-esteem and socio-economic status?* 75% of GHR said 'Yes' compared with 53% of non-GHR.

  • *Has it enabled the household to participate in the development of your community?* 62% of all respondents said 'Yes'.

  • *Has it enabled adult/social education participants to support other community members and other children in need?* Once again, there was a clear difference between responses from GHR (69%) and non-GHR (52%).

  • *Has it raised your household's level of concern for environmental issues such as soil erosion, de-forestation, pollution?* The overall 'Yes' response rate of 79% is highly encouraging, albeit within agricultural villages where this result could be anticipated. Moreover, GHR (83%) were much more likely to be aware and concerned about environmental conditions compared to non-GHR (75%).

- The findings regarding the above seven questions are strong endorsements of the power of adult/social education, notwithstanding the clear implications that the content of adult/social education matters.
- The focus of the questionnaire then moved to cultural norms and the crucial challenge of shifting entrenched norms that damage the lives of women, and particularly marginalised rural women. A series of three questions were asked where the responses could range from 'strong agreement' to 'strong disagreement', with three intermediate optional answers including 'neither agree nor disagree'. The three questions follow:

---

*More than half (53%) of all respondents **strongly disagree** that 'Marriage is more important for girls than education'.*

- *Is marriage more important for girls than education?* This is a core question in contexts of wellbeing, empowerment and equality. The findings point to transition, which implies that the value of female education is still burdened by traditional norms. By far, most respondents hold a *strong* view on this question. On the side of progress, more than half (53%) of all respondents strongly disagree that 'marriage is more important for girls than education'. On the side of tradition, one-quarter (24.7%) of all respondents strongly agree with the sentiment that 'marriage is more important for girls than education'. Expectedly, this latter response contains a gap (albeit small) between the response rates of GHR (27%) and non-GHR (23%).

67% of all household representatives strongly agreed with the proposition that education for young women should be allowed after marriage.

The second question is 'Should education for young women be allowed after marriage?' The majority (67%) of all household representatives strongly agreed that education for young women should be allowed after marriage. There is a small gap between the response rates of GHR (68%) and non-GHR (65%). 10% of all respondents strongly disagreed with the proposed question. The findings on this question corroborate the progress shown in the UNDP 2017–2018 Gender Inequality Index, where Tamil Nadu climbs into a low gender inequality category.[14]

- The third question moderates indications of progress, in the responses to whether 'young women's education and career should be decided by their parents': 83% of all respondents either strongly or somewhat agree with the sentiment that young women's education and career should be decided by their parents. 15.3% of all respondents either strongly or somewhat disagree with this norm. Readers are reminded, however, that the respondents are representative heads of households, not the young women themselves.

Focus group discussions

The intention in the focus group discussions (FGDs) was to both cross-check main survey data and provide new qualitative material on the social or community benefits (or detriments) of adult/social education. The FGDs took place with 16 village representatives/leaders of the villages selected for this study. The leadership group includes two women.

FGD facilitators asked the following questions:

1. Do you know families of women who attended Grihini classes/ courses on empowerment?
2. If 'Yes', what have these activities and programmes meant to you as village leader?
3. Have you seen changes in village life that you associate with these workshops or learning programmes?

Focus group discussion analysis

The content analysis of FGDs uses the earlier presented dimensions of wellbeing, namely capabilities and equalities. The indicators of 'capabilities' are living standard/livelihoods, health and education. The indicators of 'equalities' are self-efficacy, social actions and human rights.

Table 5.2 Profile of FGD consultants

#	Sex	Age	Ethnic/ caste community	Village	Official capacity	Occupation
1	M	48	Adivasi	AV2	Village president	Farm labourer
2	M	38	Adivasi	AV2	President of forest self-help group	Farm labourer
3	M	52	Adivasi	AV2	Village elder	Farm labourer
4	M	46	Adivasi	AV2	Village president & member of Gram Panchayat	Farm labourer
5	M	52	Sri Lankan Tamil	TSLRV	President of Colony A	Farm labourer
6	M	62	Sri Lankan Tamil	TSLRV	President of Colony C	Farm labourer
7	M	63	Sri Lankan Tamil	TSLRV	President of Colony B	Farm labourer
8	M	65	Dalit	DV2	Village president	Farm labourer
9	F	30	–	DV2	Social worker	Block development staff & women self-help group animator
10	M	40	–	DV2	Community worker	Local pastor
11	M	50	Adivasi	AV1	Village president	Farm labourer
12	M	52	Adivasi	AV1	Village elder	Farm labourer
13	M	51	Adivasi	AV1	Village elder	Farm labourer
14	M	32	Dalit	DV1	'Educated community member'	Former teacher, now businessman
15	M	30	–	DV1	Block president	Cultivator
16	F	32	Dalit	DV1	Social worker	Assistant of government social health programme

Table 5.3 shows the number of times that the responses of FGD consultants align with either capabilities or equalities indicators. This means that when a consultant's observations include related

Table 5.3 FGD content analysis word count

Wellbeing indicator	Wellbeing taxonomy	Indicator count
Self-efficacy	Equality	59
Living standard/ livelihood	Capabilities	30
Social actions	Equality	19
Human rights	Equality	18
Education	Capabilities	11
Health	Capabilities	10

expressions like 'independence', 'earning a better living', 'educating her children', 'going boldly to government offices', or 'initiating forest self-help groups', these are grouped under the designated indicators with a count of the number of times that these indicators occur during the FGDs.

What stands out in Table 5.3 is the clear recognition by participants that the Grihini programme instils values related to gender equality. This is striking, remembering that most of the village leaders/elders in the FGDs are middle-aged or older men long inculcated in patriarchal expectations. This represents a shift in the struggle for gender equalities. More specifically, the responses that align with self-efficacy are almost double those for the next most commonly observed benefit (viz. living standard/livelihood). This is not to understate the high importance rightly given by respondents to livelihood skills learned. The FGD consultants are unanimous in their associated comments about these capabilities. They commonly use words like 'self-help' to help describe thoughts about sought-after craft skills learned and social enterprise initiatives begun.

'Social action' is a crucial category of equality, as emphasised in both the statement that actions/achievements go well beyond increased feelings of self-worth and in the vision of the Beijing Declaration and Platform for Action. Evidence of social actions include the following observations:

66 *'They take loans in appropriate places for their agriculture and self-employment and pay back their loans on time.'*

'They were taught useful skills – tailoring, knitting and basket-making.'

'They have learnt skills to stand on their own legs.'
'They undertake their farming in a very effective manner and their income has increased noticeably.'
'They have built better and convenient houses.'
'They do not borrow from moneylenders.'
'Some of them can stitch for others for payment.'
'They have entrepreneurial skill and some of them have started tailoring trade.'
'[One result of the adult/social education is that] child marriage is completely gone [in the village].'
'The women understand their worth and rights.'
'The women are willing to marry other caste men also and the other caste men are willing to marry them because of their hard work and motivation.'
'They were taught many useful things – awareness, legal rights of women, numeracy and literacy...'
'They have awareness about the evils of child marriage.'
'They resist the dowry system.'
'They do not allow themselves to be exploited by upper caste people. They stand for their rights.'

'In the ASHA scheme (Assistant of Social Health Activity) among the 12 workers, 8 workers are Grihini women. They counsel pregnant women and take them to hospital for regular check-up and immunisation and accompany them for their delivery as and when needed. Graduates participate and assist in the health and other village welfare-related camps organised by government and other NGOs. Graduates have the leadership qualities to unite the rest of the villagers to address a common cause'
Female Dalit FGD consultant, Dalit. DV1 village

'They do not expect anyone's assistance in claiming their rights and benefits.'
'There is no caste discrimination openly [in the village] except the village is structured in such a way that the Dalits live in a separate location in the villages.'
'The women are not exploited.'

> *'Child marriage is not prevalent [in the village].'*
> *'Women participate and assist in the health and other village welfare-related camps organised by government and other NGOs.'*

The above observations, and those that follow depicting the multidimensionality of wellbeing, were presented by leaders of villages that have been historically damaged by caste, tribal and repatriate inequities. Their remarks evoke confidence that the social benefits of adult/social education are sufficiently influential to be able to breach oppression and invigorate the struggle for equality.

> *'Grihini is a programme for downtrodden. They know how to write petitions to various departments. They try to get their rights. Earlier they were dependent on others and now they have skills to handle their issues. There is a social change among the women in the community. The women are not exploited in the village. Child marriage is no longer prevalent.'*
> **Male Dalit FGD consultant,**
> **former teacher in DV1 village**

Notes

1 Amartya Sen (1999) *Development as Freedom.*
2 Other than indicated as the findings in text boxes, the source of data in this section is Rohan Michael Ramesh, et al. (2022) Impact of the Covid-19 National Lockdown on a Rural and Tribal Population of Tamil Nadu, Southern India: A Mixed-Methods Survey *Am J Trop Med Hyg.* 2022 Mar 16;106(5):1498–506.
3 Ibid.
4 Ibid.
5 Ibid.
6 Ibid.
7 See Swetha NB, Shobha S, Sriram S. Prevalence of catastrophic health expenditure and its associated factors, due to out-of-pocket health care expenses among households with and without chronic illness in Bangalore, India: a longitudinal study. *J Prev Med Hyg.* 2020 Apr 2;61(1):E92–E97.
8 See: tnenvis.nic.in/Database/Demography_1168.aspx?format=Print

9 Mental health and wellbeing during the Covid-19 period in Australia | ANU Centre for Social Research & Methods.

10 Saikia, et al. (2021) Covid-19, individual wellbeing and multi-dimensional poverty in the state of South Australia. PLOS ONE

11 'Self-rated health ... [is] an excellent proxy of overall health, morbidity (sickness) and mortality later in life, SRH represents a valuable tool in public health monitoring and demographic research'. See World Population. International Union for the Scientific Study of Population (IUSSP) Online News Magazine March 11, 2024. Self-rated health trends by gender and race in the USA, 1972–2018 – N-IUSSP (niussp.org)

12 Subhadip Pal and Sourav Haldar (2016), Participation and role of rural women in decision making related to farm activities: a study in Burdwan district of West Bengal, *Economic Affairs* 61(1): 55–63 March 2016 EAV61N1h.pdf (ndpublisher.in)

13 Best performing big state overall: Tamil Nadu (indiatoday.in)

14 HDI: How States Fare in Human Development. HDI: How States Fare in Human Development – CEDA (ashoka.edu.in).The finding on this question corroborates such progress.

References

Ashoka University, Centre for Economic Data and Analysis. 'HDI: How States Fare in Human Development – CEDA'. (ashoka.edu.in). (2021)

Australian National University, Centre for Social Research and Methods. Mental health and wellbeing during the Covid-19 period in Australia (2022). https://csrm.cass.anu.edu.au/research/publications/mental-health-and-wellbeing-during-covid-19-period-australia

Government of India, Ministry of Environment & Forest. (2024). tnenvis.nic.in/Database/Demography_1168.aspx?format=Print

India Today. Best Performing Big State Overall: Tamil Nadu. (27 November 2021). https://www.indiatoday.in/magazine/state-of-the-states/story/20211206-best-performing-big-state-overall-tamil-nadu-1880826-2021-11-26

International Union for the Scientific Study of Population (IUSSP). Self-rated health trends by gender and race in the USA, 1972–2018. (11 March 2024). https://www.niussp.org/health-and-mortality/self-rated-health-trends-by-gender-and-race-in-the-usa-1972-2018/

Pal, Subhadip, and Haldar, Sourav. Participation and role of rural women in decision making related to farm activities: a study in Burdwan District of West Bengal. *Economic Affairs*, March 2016; 61(1), 55–63. http://ndpublisher.in/admin/issues/EAV61N1h.pdf

Ramesh, Rohan M., Aruldas, Kumudha, Marconi, Sam D., Janagaraj, Venkateshprabhu, Rose, Anuradha, John, Sushil M., Moorthy, Mahesh, Muliyil, Jayaprakash, Saravanakumar, Puthupalayam K., Ajjampur, Sitara

S.R., and Sindhu, Kulandaipalayam N. Impact of the COVID-19 national lockdown on a rural and tribal population of Tamil Nadu, Southern India: a mixed-methods survey. *American Journal of Tropical Medicine and Hygiene*, 106(5), 1498–1506 (2022) .

Saikia, Udoy, Dodd, Melinda M., Chalmers, James, Dasvarma, Gouranga, and Schech, Susanne. COVID-19, individual wellbeing and multi-dimensional poverty in the state of South Australia. *PLOS ONE*, 16(6), e0252898 (2021).

Sen, Amartya. *Development as Freedom*. New York: Oxford University Press (1999).

Swetha NB, Shobha S, and Sriram S. Prevalence of catastrophic health expenditure and its associated factors, due to out-of-pocket health care expenses among households with and without chronic illness in Bangalore, India: a longitudinal study. *Journal of Preventive Medicine and Hygiene*, 61(1), E92–E97 (2020) .

UNDP. 'Human Development Report 2021/2022'. https://hdr.undp.org/sys tem/files/documents/global-report-document/hdr2021-22reportenglish_ 0.pdf (2021).

6 What the indices reveal in a study of marginalised women's struggle for equality in India

Wellbeing indices

An *index* refers to a composite statistic that stands for a measure of changes in a representative group of individual data points. In other words, an index is a compound measure that aggregates multiple indicators, thereby summarising and ranking specific observations. Its usefulness in this research is to show the development of a calculated number over time by showing the change of the number from one point in time to another. In sum, index numbers simplify otherwise complex comparisons.

The selection of capabilities and equalities indicators relies on the need to reflect the fundamental capabilities of human development and empowerment, to support the conceptual grounds of the study and to build an ability to influence policy change.

The details of the methodology used for this research's twin indices (capabilities and equalities) are recorded in Appendix 2. In brief: three indicators are selected from each of the three components of the 'capabilities' and 'equalities' dimensions, respectively. The three dimensions of capabilities in the questionnaire are living standard/ livelihoods, health and education. The three dimensions of equalities are self-efficacy, social actions and human rights. The nine indicators in each index comprise responses from both Grihini and non-Grihini participants.

Side note: in the following bar graphs that represent the interview data, the percentage of individual respondents shown to have achieved wellbeing means that from the combined dimensions they achieved the requisite score in the aggregate.

DOI: 10.4324/9781003519409-6

Capabilities index

As Figure 6.1. shows, 76.7% of all women respondents achieved well-being in the capabilities index, and almost one-quarter of all women (23.3%) have not yet achieved wellbeing in this index.

Failure to achieve wellbeing in capabilities means deprivations in one or more areas of living standard, health and/or education. The drivers of deprivation are discussed in the next section.

Drivers of capabilities

Figures 6.2, 6.3 and 6.4 show that health is the key driver of wellbeing in capabilities (85%).

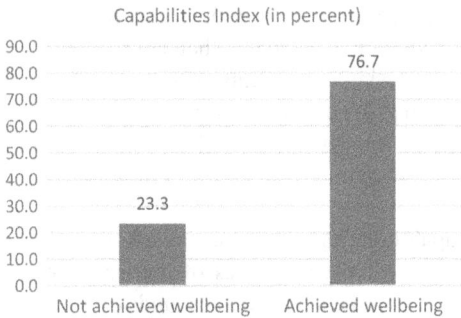

Figure 6.1 Capabilities index.

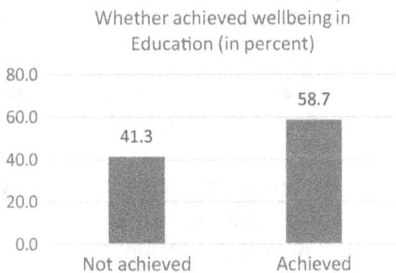

Figure 6.2 Whether achieved wellbeing in education.

Whether achieved wellbeing in Health
(in percent)

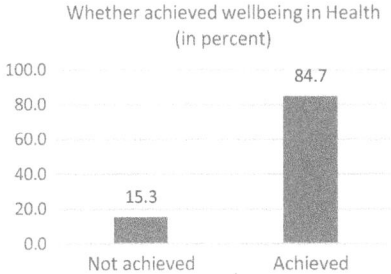

Figure 6.3 Whether achieved wellbeing in health.

Whether achieved wellbeing
in Living standard /
Livelihoods (in percent)

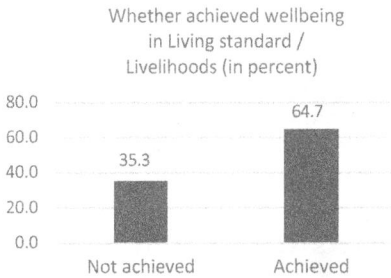

Figure 6.4 Whether achieved wellbeing in living standard/livelihood.

Conversely, education is where *most* women have not yet achieved wellbeing. Note that education surveys not just achievement level, but also constraints on education and access to internet. The significance of education deprivations is discussed in the Summary section of Chapter Seven.

The next lowest achievement of wellbeing in the capabilities index is in living standards/livelihoods. Respondents scored relatively better in health. On the other hand, any respondent deprived in any of these dimensions belongs to a category of concern for public policy interventions.

Equalities Index (in percent)

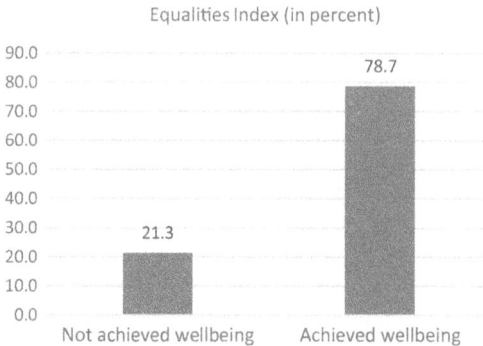

Figure 6.5 Equalities index.

Equalities index

Just over three-quarters of all women respondents (78.7%) achieved wellbeing in the equalities index; 21.3% have not yet experienced wellbeing in equalities.

Any inequality is clearly an issue. At the same time, readers are reminded that the value of indices is the picture that they show over time. Has there been improvement? Or is there slippage?

Drivers of equalities

Figures 6.6, 6.7 and 6.8 show that the dimension where most women achieved wellbeing in equalities is social actions (87%), followed by self-efficacy (74%).

Human rights is the main driver of *lack* of wellbeing in equalities (51%). Human rights questions include safety/security. This makes human rights a finding of high concern given previously discussed data on violence in the family. This said, there is an implication of progress in the finding that just under 50% of women did achieve wellbeing in human rights. As discussed, this is partly influenced by data on the percentage of women (56%) who do *not* experience violence in the family.

After human rights, the next most prevalent driver of lack of equality involves self-efficacy. This is measured by indicators that include participation in decision-making and confidence in communicating / public speaking. These are areas where the beneficiaries

Whether achieved wellbeing in social
actions (in percent)

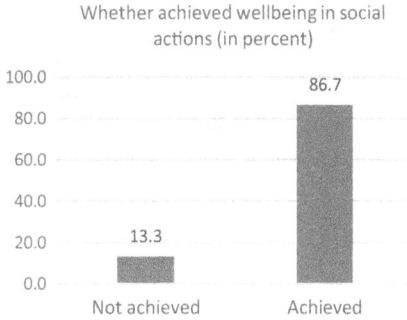

Figure 6.6 Whether achieved wellbeing in social actions.

Whether achieved wellbeing
in self efficacy (in
percent)

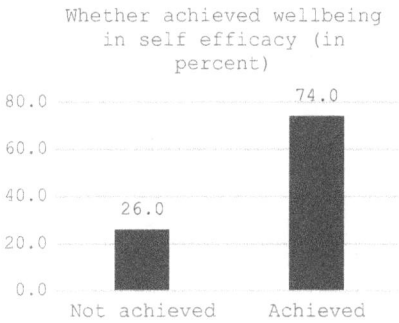

Figure 6.7 Whether achieved wellbeing in self-efficacy.

Whether achieved wellbeing in human
rights (in percent)

Figure 6.8 Whether achieved wellbeing in human rights.

of adult/social education at the Grihini programme were much more likely to achieve wellbeing. As noted previously, 58% of Grihini graduates reported 'excellent' capability in public speaking, compared to 48% of respondents who have not engaged with adult/social education. The third area in the equalities index is social actions. A strong number of women did achieve wellbeing in this dimension – almost 87% of all women respondents.

7 Prologue of an investigation of marginalised women's struggle for equality in India

Summary

In recent years, there has been increased focus on research of different dimensions of social disadvantage, particularly from longitudinal and gender perspectives, in the context of public policy. This happens especially in research that conceptualises and measures the multiple dimensions of wellbeing or quality of life. The cornerstone in this field of research is the Gender Inequality Index that uses three dimensions: reproductive health, empowerment and the labour market. More recent is the Gender Social Norms Index that uses four dimensions (political, educational, economic and physical integrity) to tackle the undervaluation of and constraints on women's capabilities, rights and opportunities in society. Both these indices cover global populations. Importantly, this enables countries to compare and contrast their policy performance longitudinally.

At the same time, and what makes this book more relevant now than ever before, is the fact that the focus of governance is changing. There is increasing demand on policymakers for *local*-level evidence on the multiple factors of empowerment and wellbeing (quality of life) in the relations between gender inequalities and deprivations. This demand is fuelled by evidentiary need for neighbourhood-level data to explain why women and girls continue to face discrimination and lack of opportunities in the workplace, education and healthcare. This is especially the case when disaggregated data contest country- and state-level data that ostensibly signal progress towards achieving the Sustainable Development Goals.

The starting point for analysis of equalities is the understanding that wellbeing and empowerment are interconnected by capabilities

DOI: 10.4324/9781003519409-7

that go beyond increased feelings of self-worth. This aligns with the vision of the Beijing Declaration and Platform for Action which imagines a world where every woman and girl can exercise her capabilities and actions. Such actions signify living free from violence, engaging in decisions concerning one's own life, gaining the same affordable access as men and boys to good healthcare and education, and benefiting from opportunities to work that parallel those of men.

The approach in this book interrogates the forceful role of adult/ social education in women's efforts to achieve equality. The analysis presents examples of the dynamic influence of social education. Significantly, these include the development of livelihood skills that make it possible to avoid cross-generational debt, and empowerment that enables ability to claim human rights through breaching traditions of violence such as child marriage.

Turning to the findings measured by the twin wellbeing indices of capabilities and equalities, it was shown that 77% of the 150 interview participants *did* achieve the benchmark score for wellbeing in the capabilities index. Conversely, almost one-quarter of the respondents have *not* yet achieved wellbeing in capabilities. Education is the dimension with the greatest deprivation, where *most* women did not achieve wellbeing. The education section of the survey tool comprises questions that include level of schooling, constraints on education, and access to internet. (The significance of education deprivations is discussed further below.) The next lowest achievement of wellbeing in the capabilities index is in living standard/livelihoods. Respondents scored relatively better in health.

Shifting to the equalities index findings: 79% of all women respondents achieved wellbeing in the equalities index. Conversely, 21% have *not* yet experienced wellbeing in equalities. The main driver of achieving equalities in this study is social actions (87%). As a definitive quality of empowerment in this study, it is significant that 131 of 150 women achieved wellbeing in this crucial area of empowerment. The second strongest driver of wellbeing in equalities is self-efficacy, where just under three-quarters of the women achieved wellbeing.

Most of the lack of wellbeing in equalities (51%) is driven by deprivations in human rights, which in the survey includes safety/ security. On the other hand, it is important to note that just under 50% of women *did* achieve wellbeing in human rights. Again, this corroborates the finding that 56% of all women in the study do *not* experience violence in the family.

Following human rights, the second most prevalent driver of lack of wellbeing in equalities is self-efficacy. This is measured by indicators that include participation in decision-making and confidence in communicating / public speaking. Significantly, these are areas where the beneficiaries of adult/social education are much more likely to achieve wellbeing in self-efficacy. As previously noted, 58% of Grihini graduates reported 'excellent' capability in public speaking, compared to 48% of respondents who have not engaged in adult/ social education.

Turning to the question of the contribution of the study, the key question is: how does the research promote the efforts of rural marginalised women towards equality in Tamil Nadu? The impacts of this research proceed from a wellbeing approach designed to expose the compound dimensions of women's capability and empowerment. The key proposition in the theory hinges on the detail that if empowerment is not present in wellbeing, then it becomes a severely weakened version of wellbeing. With wellbeing being contingent on equality, the methodology depicts the intersection of capabilities and empowerment/agency.

Adult/social education of the Grihini kind that is investigated in this book belongs to a strong legacy of consciousness-raising or *defamiliarisation*. 'Defamiliarization' means making normalised things intolerable by seeing them from a different angle, through a different lens.[1] In the various different contexts where adult/social education takes place, there is a shared expectation that agent-oriented learning approaches focused on power relations could help to transform structural oppression. There are well-known examples of successful social transformation in the work of Gramsci, Habermas, Freire and the American feminist movement.

The research presents illustrations of how this methodology uncovers some of the gains that marginalised rural women have made towards equality – as well as the remorseless obstacles and unjust conditions. For example, serious challenges show up in income inequality for formally educated women – a known adversity in Tamil Nadu that is called 'education unemployment'. Tackling this is a crucial policy need. At the same time, the research methodology is formulated to highlight the manifold realities of inequality beyond the workplace. They need to be tackled by public policy actions in their entirety, through targeted interventions grounded in recurrent data collection.

Adult/social education plays a significant role in the proposed interventions. The anecdotal evidence in this study is compelling: empowerment education is a force in the struggle for emancipation. For example, Grihini adult/social education graduates (35%) are much more likely to go alone outside the village most of the time compared with non-GR participants (24%). This act of empowerment is an important achievement, considering patriarchal socio-cultural contexts. Still, 'empowerment' is an over-used expression, which the research addresses by giving it special characteristics. 'Empowerment' is defined in this book on the basis of evidence that a woman has acquired and realised social action capabilities that go beyond a sense of empowerment. These capabilities imply literacy that is functional but also enables enactment of agency or self-efficacy, in the struggle for equality. An example in the study of the enactment of such empowerment is where 58% of Grihini graduate women self-report 'excellent' capability in the sphere of public speaking / being able to influence others including public officials.

Alongside the subjective benefits of adult/social education, the methodology casts light on the *social reach* of individual empowerment, meaning its influence on collective wellbeing. An example of this is shown by the finding that almost one-third of Grihini graduates attended a village or town meeting or discussion on gender inequality and/or environmental concerns in the past 12 months. This represents a high rate of social action and prospective emancipation. It stands out strongly in comparison with most country contexts in the global south *or* north. Anecdotal evidence of this is presented from interviews conducted with village leaders/elders, which include the following observations:

66 *'The women have the leadership qualities to unite the rest of the villagers to address a common cause.'*

'They help the other villagers in need.'

'They resist the dowry system.'

'They have awareness about the evils of child marriage.'

'The women are willing to marry other caste men also and the other caste men are willing to marry them because of their hard work and motivation.'

'They have knowledge in legal rights.'

While a picture emerges of the intersecting benefits of adult/social education for both individual women and the village, this does not obscure the unmistakable support of elders/leaders for the individual emancipation of the women in their villages. Indeed, the village leaders' observations show deep appreciation of and admiration for the women:

> *'Women participate and assist in the health and other village welfare-related camps organised by government and other NGOs.'*

66 *'Knowledge gives them confidence.'*
'They do not expect others to help them, and they think and take decision, which they think is appropriate.'
'They have learnt skills to stand on their own legs.'
'They have entrepreneurial skill and some of them have started tailoring trade.'
'They do not allow themselves to be exploited by upper caste people.'
'They stand for their rights.'
'The women are not exploited [in the village].'

Regarding the details of the elders' appreciation, they note how they are moved by the women's socio-legal understanding of the struggle. They comment on how adult/social education helps them to negate the dowry system, child marriage, and caste- and ethnicity-based discrimination in their villages. While such observations touch on very powerful socio-cultural obstacles and oppressive conditions that persist for many rural marginalised women in Tamil Nadu, the study uncovers significant evidence of resistance. For example, 69% of all women respondents maintain a man is *not* justified in hitting or beating a woman in the household if she argues with him.

There are state laws that prohibit some forms of discrimination faced by Scheduled Caste and Scheduled Tribe communities. There is a law that addresses violence and another that criminalises untouchability practices. A workplace example of the latter forbids employers from favouring/privileging a particular social class or race.

Regrettably, both state laws are ill-practised, which means that very few legal cases are filed in a year in Tamil Nadu.[2]

The research explores the ramifications of workplace discrimination in terms of 'education unemployment'. What it helps to show is that the Dravidian movement has eked out crucial gains in education and literacy, and yet educated marginalised women are still unable to get appropriate work. In the unlikely scenario that a woman 'succeeds' in gaining such work, she is underpaid. Predictably, educated women tend to withdraw from the labour force when there is no option of suitable jobs.[3] Indications of 'retreat' are visible in responses to a question that asks women: 'Have you done any work other than your housework in the past 12 months?' 35% of all respondents said they had not. Of the 'Yes' respondents, one-third reported that they were not paid, either in cash or kind. To restate their qualifications for good jobs, almost 50% of the women self-report an *advanced* ability in reading and writing in Tamil; 20% said they also have *advanced* skills in English, while another 20% said their English skills were *intermediate*. These are strong statistics in any country's rural context.

Ultimately, wellbeing approaches have a special interest in people who have *not* yet achieved wellbeing. It is this group who need to be the special concern of public policymakers. In the case of education achievements, the research points up a concerning fact that 18% of all women respondents 'never completed any education'.

Absence of education correlates with income poverty, as discussed in the analysis of living standards / subsistence data. Recognition of this correlation is not new. This shows up in the current India Census (2011) which records a significant literacy gap between rural women (71%) and urban women (86%). In other words, this disparity was already apparent 12 years ago.[4] This is also true of additional gender literacy disparities that disfavour the rural population. Notably, rural female literacy is 65%, compared with 82% in male counterparts.[5]

In short, rural women in Tamil Nadu face inequalities beyond 'education unemployment'. This is a recurrent finding that surfaces in the study's multidimensional approach. Tackling multidimensional inequalities necessitates data beyond job figures, earnings, or level of education. Special methods are needed to formulate public policy solutions beyond economic productivity and social engineering. Targeting is essential, as is the periodic calculation of quality-of-life data. The value of indices lies in their longitudinal worth, but even this one study makes it evident that rural women without any education are an essential target group. Among other target groups are rural marginalised women without their own means of transport, in regions where public transport is uncommon. 27% of all women respondents in this study of the Palni Hills do not own a motor scooter or motorbike.

To 'leave no person behind' conveys the overarching intent of public policy in Tamil Nadu. This can be inferred from the official mantra of Unity and Equality.[6] It is expressed at high political levels, as seen in the remarks of Chief Minister Stalin in his address to the 2023 National Conference of All India Federation: 'The struggle for the attainment of social justice [...] is associated with the structure of Indian society'.[7] This public policy concern for equality gives rise to the question of how this study of the Palni Hills might contribute to wider public policy interventions.

There is a bigger national context that matters a lot and where the question of this study's wider contribution is evident. This involves India's intent to achieve its 'demographic dividend' – a term that refers to the extraordinary potential for India, as the world's most populous country, to generate a human capability dividend from the expanded percentage of the population who 'actively seek work'. If the country fails to develop people's human capabilities through good jobs, there will be an inflated dependency ratio that entails economically dependent people.[8]

The provision of good jobs is a very big challenge because the country's strong economic growth to date has largely been 'jobless economic growth.'[9] On the other hand, there is a clear starting point: India's female labour participation rate is very low. The Center for Monitoring the Indian Economy uses a restrictive definition of employment but still finds that only 10% of working-age Indian women in 2022 are either employed or looking for jobs.[10] Achieving the demographic dividend depends on urgent transformation of educated unemployment.

To what extent could adult/social education contribute to the achievement of the demographic dividend? As well as being a fundamental component of wellbeing as this research shows, adult/social education is a prerequisite of *doing* good jobs. The anecdotal evidence collected in this book presents two manifold reasons for this: first, empowerment gained through adult/social education helps motivate women to seek good jobs; and second, the curriculum of adult/social education develops essential strong workplace capabilities. Examples include communication, interpersonal skills, problem solving, critical thinking, teamwork and time management. These are visible in the comments of village elders. Examples of their remarks bear repeating (below) since they highlight the definitive importance of empowerment, which stems from but goes beyond heightened valuation of self:

66 *'Women go on their own to respective government offices for various schemes they are entitled for.'*
'They go up to the District Collector's office without outside help.'
'The women talk to the government and other officials boldly.'

Her stories

Ten women presented their stories on the phone. Reported below, they illustrate the women's reflections on what adult/social education means to them.

I am from Paliyar tribal community and my native place is a remote village in the lower hills of Kodaikanal. I have studied only up to fifth grade. At Grihini, I was taught to read and write and I obtained skills in tailoring, knitting, basket making and handicrafts. I learnt to stitch sari blouse and dresses for small children. I started eating vegetables, cereals, fruits and greens. I did not know the value of vegetables. I learnt from Grihini vegetables are very important for our growth, health and stamina. I understood that my village has lot of vegetables and my neighbourhood has valuable herbs and fruits. The exposure I had at Grihini motivated me to educate my children. My daughter has completed her B.Com. My elder son is a supervisor in a leather company at Chennai. He has training to make shoes. My younger son is in ninth grade. There are noticeable changes in my village and the Grihini alumni are particular to educate their children. If I had not had the training at Grihini, I would not have educated my children.

📞 *I am from a remote village in the lower hills of Kodaikanal. At Grihini I took classes on how to conduct debates. They would divide us into groups and give various topics to conduct debates. This helped me to give talks in public forums boldly and eloquently. In awareness classes, motivational videos were shown and people without limbs performed marvellous things for others and took care of themselves. This helped me to be motivated and take challenges in life to live a meaningful and productive life and be of help to others. In environmental classes, I learnt how human beings are irresponsible in polluting the air, water and land for their own advantages. In my village, I have explained to people how trees are important for rain and how we must be responsible in keeping the nature protected which is the life source for all living things. I have told my family members and relatives that the tree should not be cut for firewood and for other reasons.*

📞 *My native place is a village in lower hills of Kodaikanal. I failed my 10th grade government exam and I could not continue my education. Hence, I joined Grihini. When I saw other students like me have completed their 12th grade, I also wanted to study and complete my 12th grade. I completed my 12th grade at Grihini and I joined the one-year diploma course in multi-disability rehabilitation. This course motivated me work for the children with intellectual disabilities. I took B.A. through correspondence and completed my B.Ed. also. Grihini gave me the courage, motivation and the passion for education. My desire to help the children with intellectual disabilities is possible because of the training I had at Grihini. I got a teaching position at the local government high school to instruct the students with intellectual disabilities. Though my salary is low, the joy and the satisfaction I get is enormous. In my village children would not go to school regularly, most of them go for day labouring. I encourage the children of my village to go to school. After seeing me, some of my relatives are determined to educate their children.*

I am from a village belonging to Dalit (Mathari) community. In my village there were situations where boys had more privileges and enjoyed higher status. Only boys were encouraged to study and when food was served from the cooking pot the top portion of the food was given to boys and the lower portion of the food to the girls. It was expected that women should be subservient to men and they cannot make any decision. Men could be drunkards and womanisers but women cannot question any of their vices. The Dalit community people were treated as dirt and should subject themselves to all sorts of atrocities of their own men plus the men of other castes. The students were very poor and most of us were Dalits and Tribals. The leaders of Grihini treated us with respect and dignity. The awareness classes and talks opened my eyes and I understood that a woman is a mighty person and she is capable of running her family in an efficient manner and can think and function independently. When a man did wrong things the women have all the rights to question him. The labourers should not be paid based on their caste but on their performance. When a farm owner paid me less than the other women did I fought with him and got equal salary. I learnt tailoring, knitting, handicrafts and pickle and jam making. The tailoring helped me to get a tailoring teacher job in one of the towns in the plains. I enrolled in a correspondence course and finished B.A. I share my skills and knowledge that I acquired from Grihini to my village people. My husband had an affair with a woman and left the children and me high and dry. I was shattered. My daughters were young and it was not easy but I did not lose hope. The teachings and exposure I had at Grihini strengthen me to face the challenges and find a way to come out them. The tailoring skills that Grihini gave helped me to earn a livelihood. Now I have a nursery teacher's job and I have educated my daughters well. My first daughter has completed her MBA and my second daughter is doing her first year M.Sc. in Chemistry.

I am from a tribal community and I come from a remote village in the lower hills of Kodaikanal. The meaning of my village is 'last of the forest'. I joined Grihini in 1990 and it was a new world to me. I was terrified of people whom I do not know and I was scared to meet new people. The training and exposure I had at Grihini helped me to gain confidence and motivation. I had training in tailoring, basket making, knitting and handicrafts. I had a special interest in knitting and I could make fine woollen caps, scarves and sweaters. I was not aware of the natural vegetables, greens and fruits available in my neighbourhood and the importance of them in providing immunity and strength. The most important learning I had in Grihini was the importance of education. I was determined to educate my children. My daughter has finished her B.Sc. and my son is in 12th grade. My daughter is working in a government scheme, which teaches the children from home. When children of my village do not go to school regularly I counselled their parents and explained to them the importance of education and motivate them to send their children to schools regularly. I can proudly say that the valuable education I had at Grihini has empowered me to be a Panchayat Ward Member in my village.

I am from TSLRV (Sri Lankan Repatriates). I had studied only up to eighth grade [when] I joined Grihini programme. The awareness songs, skits and classes that were taught in Grihini made me to understand the structure of the society based on caste and religion. I understood the position of women in the society and how they are exploited, oppressed, and denied some of their basic rights. I have gone to jail for participating in the strike, demanding road to my village. Grihini has equipped me with skills and knowledge to read and write fluently and address in the public forums confidently, constructively and authentically. If I had not come to Grihini, I would have been a life-long day labourer and wasted my talents and potential. My daughter is doing her second-year bachelor's degree in mathematics and my son is in 12th grade. My husband is a motor mechanic.

📞 *I am from a village where each caste has its own location. From the location, the caste of its residents can be identified. After I finished my studies at Grihini, I worked in the Unorganised Labor Welfare Union scheme of PEAK also. Grihini has given me skills to organise public meetings within a short time and run them efficiently. I have the confidence to talk in public forums. I take tuition to the children of self-help group women. I encourage the parents of my village to send their children to school regularly. I prepare woollen things and pickles for sale and I get good income from the sale. I am the group leader for the Kurinjimalar self-help welfare programme in my village. I am the vice president of the managing committee of the local school. I am married and have two lovely children. My daughter wants to become a professor and my son to become an auditor. My husband works in micro finance scheme.*

📞 *I am from a village in the Upper Hills of Kodaikanal. I was extremely shy and timid. I found it difficult to go away from my village. The homely and unthreatening environment in the Grihini helped me to fit in easily and quickly. The skills and the personality development I received at Grihini has equipped me to have two jobs. I am a government Balwadi teacher and a teacher in an after school care programme of an NGO. I can talk to people boldly, go to different places alone and meet the officials. I can conduct myself with dignity and respect. I was determined to get a decent livelihood of my own and not to depend on my parents or siblings.*

📞 *I come from a remote village where most of the people are illiterates and uncultured. Those days women were subservient to men and they could not any decision on their own. I came from a village and I did not a have clue how to mingle with others and how to conduct myself with other students of my age. The most important things that I learnt is that education is the integral part of life and my daughter has completed her M.Sc. and my son has done information rational technology course and he work in Infosys. In my village, I help the pregnant women to have nutritious food, timely medical check-up from a qualified gynaecologist. I guide and motivate the women of my village to be self-confident and independent. I participate in all the events of my village and people seek my guidance.*

I am from a village belonging to Paliyar tribe. I was a very shy and timid person and I would not volunteer to answer in classes and participate in discussions. The training I had at Grihini give me motivation and confidence to talk boldly and be assertive. The training helps me to think and take right decisions. Like some of my young village girls, I am not in a hurry to get married. I want to have adequate emotional and physical maturity before I get married. I have bought a sewing machine and I earn good income from stitching blouses and chudhidhars.

Discussion of graduate narratives

Overall, the narratives above are a compelling supplement to the survey data that enable readers to gain a deeper understanding of the complexity of empowerment that includes constructs such as confidence, decision-making, skills for navigating life challenges and the capacity to help themselves and engage productively with others.

The detailed analysis of the wellbeing survey has provided a broad scope and depth of information about the current status of the women's lives in these five research villages, triangulating the views of the different stakeholders, namely the women, their household representatives and village leaders. It has also provided a comparison of wellbeing of the graduates with those women who have not had the

Kodaikanal Grihini education experience. Some comparisons have been somewhat challenging and unexpected and give cause to reconsider any taken-for-granted assumptions about the diverse impacts of education. Surprising, for example, is the finding that 25.3% of Grihini respondents report that they do *not* participate in decisions about how their earnings will be used, compared to 11.1% of non-Grihini respondents. More surprising again is the finding on Grihini graduates' concerns about family violence. The data show that 49.4% of Grihini graduates suffer emotionally or physically from violence in the family, which is a distinctly higher number than those (36.5%) in the non-Grihini cohort. The unexpected result could be attributed to the facts that: 1) violence has been normalised within villages and households; and 2) the Grihini intervention of social education and social literacy has made what has been normalised to feel wrong once Grihini students had the opportunity to consider it from another viewpoint. In other words, they were more critically aware of the injustice of violence against women.

More generally, what is apparent and confirms the survey's findings is that the women have come to understand that the challenges they experience are not merely their own personal lot in life but are injustices that are experienced by poor and marginalised women who have their human and citizen rights denied. They also understand that there is a need for them to be proactive in changing their current status and oppressive experiences *and those of all the women in their village.* The narratives reveal that the graduates have gained the courage to think critically about situated problems and have gained the confidence in their ability to make the 'right decisions' for the betterment not only of themselves but of others and the environment. The Grihini experience has provided them with hope and aspirations that they translate into gaining employment and seeking a better future for their children. They also are prepared to negotiate a liveable wage as well as to negotiate with government officials for the basic services their village needs, such as roads and electricity.

Two impacts that show up in the narratives are especially notable. One is Grihini graduates' willingness to pass on their learning to other women in the village, for example, to encourage young women to gain an education, to resist early marriage and to seek good nutrition when pregnant. The other is that they have learned the importance of early education. They ensure that their own children attend school and even to go on to further education to gain employability skills, and they encourage other parents in the village to send their children to school. This study was initiated to gain an understanding of the impact that 37 years of continuous women's education at the Kodaikanal Grihini programme has had on its graduates, their families and their villages. The Grihini education programme prioritised young women who were from the Dalit and Adivasi villages as well as girls from repatriated Tamil communities who came from war-torn Sri Lanka only to become bonded labourers upon arrival in India. The recruiting focused on selecting those who were the most poor and marginalised members in their village. Internal and external evaluations of the effectiveness of, and satisfaction with, the Grihini programme have occurred on a regular basis over time and were used to adjust the programme to meet the changing and diverse needs of the young women from these villages. However, it is important to note that this study is not an evaluation study but an impact study. The difference lies in turning the gaze to focus on wellbeing in the lives of its key stakeholders rather than on the nature, quality and operations of features of the programme.

A key learning from the detailed findings is that the women still face challenges in these villages: they still face lack of access to adequate healthcare, and they still face oppression, discrimination, hunger and violence. However, what is different is that they have learned to face these challenges with a sense of their own worth and their entitlement to respect within their families, within their village, from those who employ them and from those who provide government services.

There is not a common starting point for all the students, and some young women complete a year's programme still needing to acquire basic knowledge and skills. However, they all leave with a sense of their own responsibility to make decisions about how to confront their problems. They also leave with a sense of personal social obligation to seek wellbeing not only for themselves but for their families, their community and the environment. They readily use their new-found knowledge and skills to speak confidently, respectfully and assertively to government officers to gain benefits for their villages, and are able to seek better work conditions and wages for themselves. In short, Grihini graduates have become both formal and informal leaders in their villages who are trusted to work for the common good. Above all, they have learned the value and importance of education and are advocates for children attending school.

Gaining hope, happiness, aspiration and achievement has been a catalyst for the graduates' wellbeing and contributed to enhanced wellbeing in their families and their villages where hope, aspiration and social action occur. However, the impact study demonstrates that despite these improvements, sustainable large-scale social change will take more time.

What was important to find is that there is congruence between the Grihini graduates' responses and those of the household and village leaders. An early concern of the programme was that there was a risk that when the graduates returned to their villages as more literate, assertive and confident young women, they might be rejected by their villages. However, the household heads and village leaders have confirmed that there has been a quite different outcome. Importantly, they express their appreciation of the accord that the graduates have brought to the villages through their respect for difference and their readiness to work for the betterment of the community.

The Kodaikanal Grihini programme began with AUS$6,000. It was supported with AUS$10,000 per annum for approximately eight years, increasing over time to AUS$35,000. Over the last 10 years the cost has fluctuated between AUS$60,000 and AUS$80,000 as a registered Community College. However, since COVID, there has been a return to a more focused programme that aims to ensure women's social awareness, employability and functional literacy, which costs around AUS$40,000 per annum. For this meagre sum, well over 2,000 girls from remote villages who had not gained or completed their education have graduated the Grihini programme with functional and social literacy and with skills to gain employment or establish their own enterprise. In addition, 30 girls and young women have received education awards that have enabled them to go on to further study in community colleges and universities to graduate as nurses, teachers, social workers or with arts or science degrees.

Notes

1 In the context of skits used in adult education, Bertolt Brecht would have recognised methods he called the *alienation effect* or *distancing effect* in efforts to distance adult learners from emotional involvement in the skits through jarring reminders of everyday inequalities.
2 Prabu (2020) Tackling Caste Discrimination Through the Law-Madurai Talks Among CSOs – Centre for Law & Public Policy Research (clpr.org.in)

3 See Rural development and gender equality: A reality check in Tamil Nadu (downtoearth.org.in)
4 Indian States by Literacy Rate 2024 | Literacy Rate in India (www.finde asy.in)
5 Govt of India (2023) www.tnenvis.nic.in/Database/Demography_1168. aspx?format=Print
6 'Struggle for attaining social justice is not a matter for just a single state': Tamil Nadu CM Stalin – ThePrint – ANIFeed
7 Ibid.
8 This refers to the average number of economically dependent population per 100 economically productive population. See Dependency ratio (who. int)
9 See 42546020.pdf (oecd.org)
10 As India's population soars, number of women in workforce shrinks | Women's Rights News | Al Jazeera

References

Al Jazeera. As India's Population Soars, Number of Women in Workforce Shrinks. (10 April 2023). www.aljazeera.com/gallery/2023/4/10/as-indias-population-soars-number-of-women-in-workforce-shrinks
Down to Earth. Rural development and gender equality: a reality check in Tamil Nadu. (6 January 2020). https://www.downtoearth.org.in/blog/governance/rural-development-and-gender-equality-a-reality-check-in-tamil-nadu-68678
FindEasy. Indian States by Literacy Rate 2024 | Literacy Rate in India. www.findeasy.in/indian-states-by-literacy-rate/
Government of India. Demography of Tamil Nadu. (2023). www.tnenvis.nic.in/Database/Demography_1168.aspx?format=Print
Kundu, Amitabh, and Mohanan, P. Chikkamuni. Employment and Inequality Outcomes in India. OECD. www.oecd.org/employment/emp/42546020.pdf
Prabu, C. Tackling Caste Discrimination Through the Law-Madurai Talks Among CSOs. Centre for Law & Public Policy Research (2020). https://clpr.org.in/blog/tackling-caste-discrimination-through-the-law-csos-training-workshop-at-madurai/
The Print. 'Struggle for attaining social justice is not a matter for just a single state': Tamil Nadu CM Stalin. (4 April 2023). https://theprint.in/india/struggle-for-attaining-social-justice-is-not-a-matter-for-just-a-single-state-tamil-nadu-cm-stalin/1494968/
World Health Organization. Dependency ratio. www.who.int/data/gho/indicator-metadata-registry/imr-details/3441

Appendices

Appendix 1. Areas of life measured

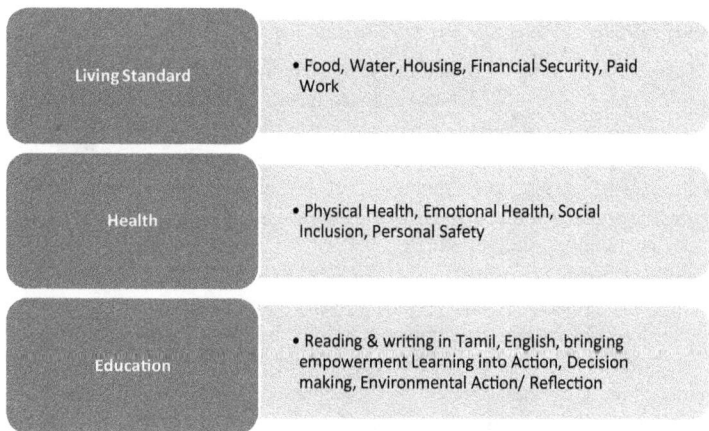

Living Standard	• Food, Water, Housing, Financial Security, Paid Work
Health	• Physical Health, Emotional Health, Social Inclusion, Personal Safety
Education	• Reading & writing in Tamil, English, bringing empowerment Learning into Action, Decision making, Environmental Action/ Reflection

Figure A.1 Areas of life measured.

Appendix 2. Index indicators

Capabilities index indicators

Living standard/livelihoods dimension

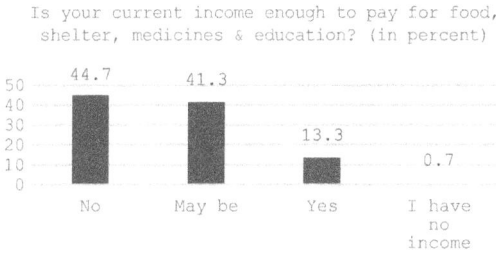

Figure A.2 Sufficient income for food, shelter, medicines & education.

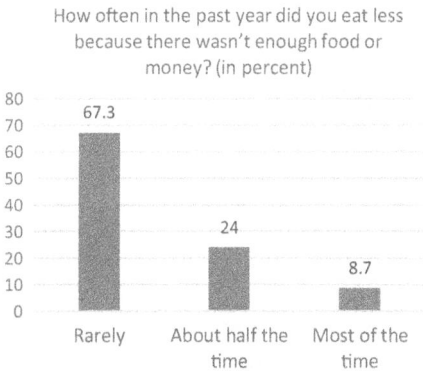

Figure A.3 Eating less due to insufficient food/money in past year.

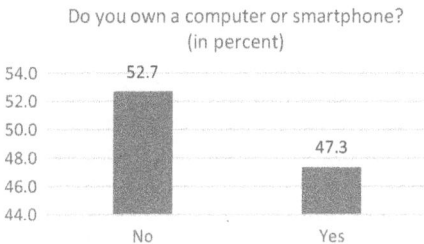

Figure A.4 Owns a computer or smartphone.

Health dimension

On the whole, how would you rate your physical
health? (in percent)

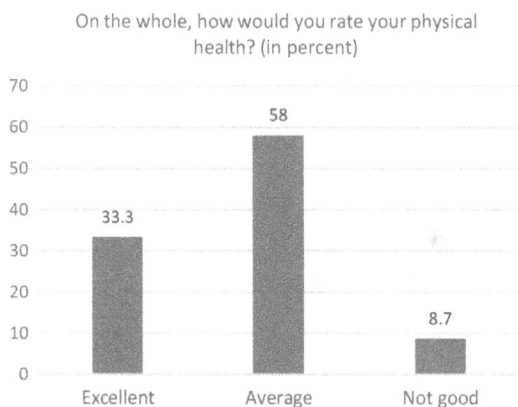

Figure A.5 Self-reported assessment of physical health.

Have you had a long-lasting illness that lasted over
six months? (in percent)

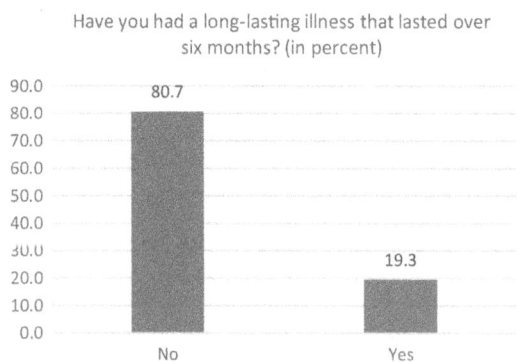

Figure A.6 Illness that lasted over six months.

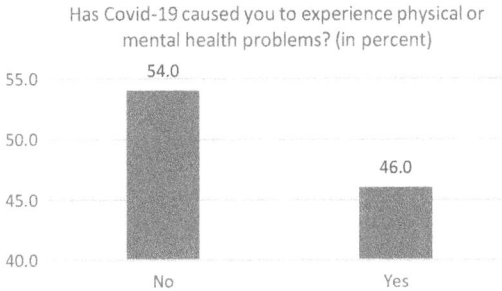

Figure A.7 Physical or mental problems from COVID-19.

Education dimension

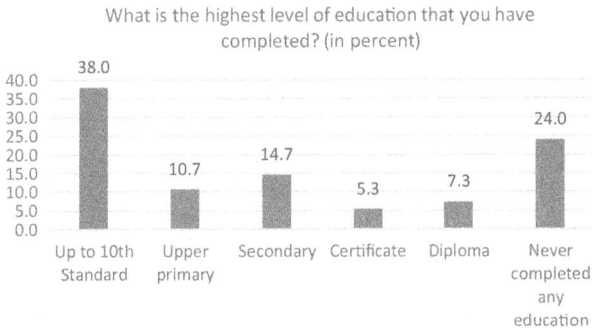

Figure A.8 Highest education level completed.

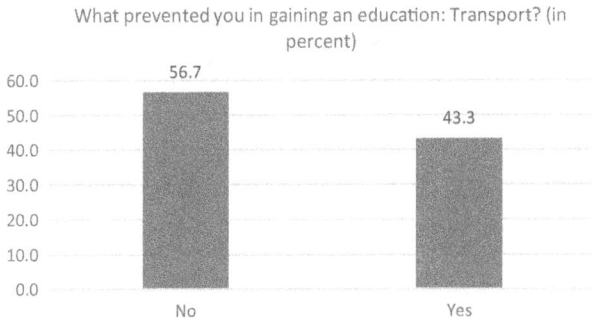

Figure A.9 Transport as a barrier to education.

What is your level of reading and writing in TAMIL? (in percent)

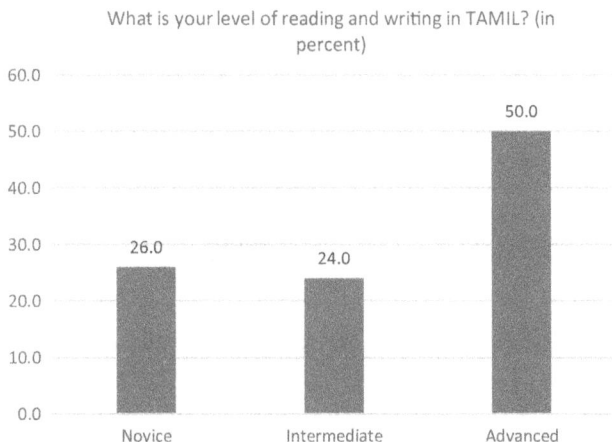

Figure A.10 Level of literacy in Tamil.

Equalities index indicators

Self-efficacy dimension

Do you usually go alone to the Market? (in percent)

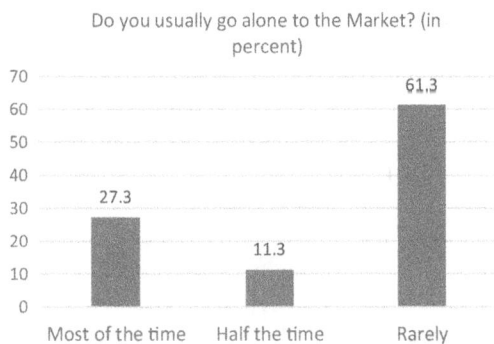

Figure A.11 Able to go alone to the market?

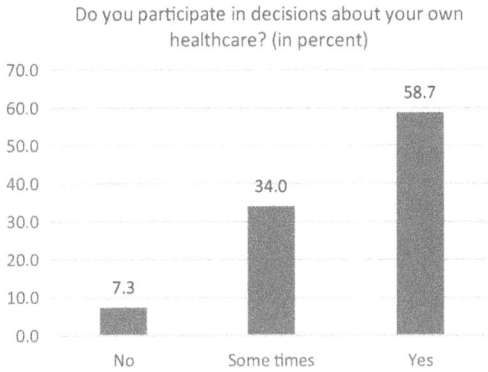

Figure A.12 Participation in own healthcare decisions.

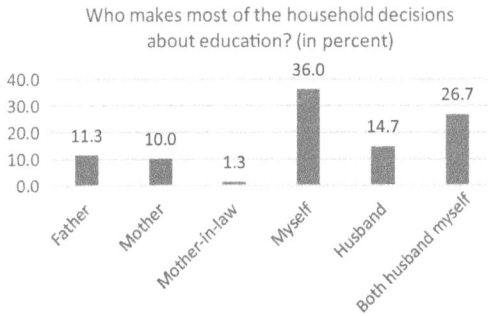

Figure A.13 Key household decision-maker about education.

Social actions dimension

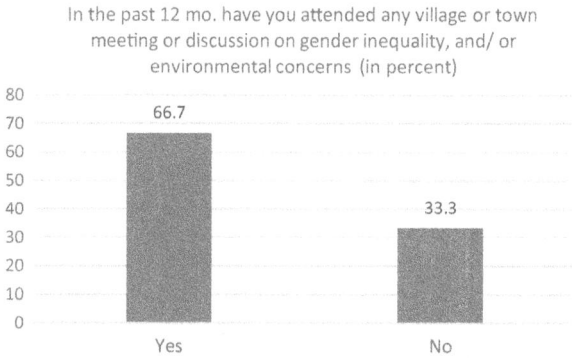

Figure A.14 Attended meetings on inequality/environment in past year.

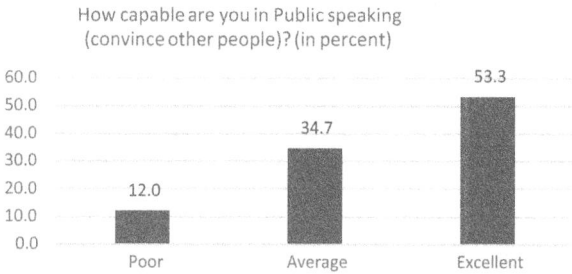

Figure A.15 Capability in public speaking.

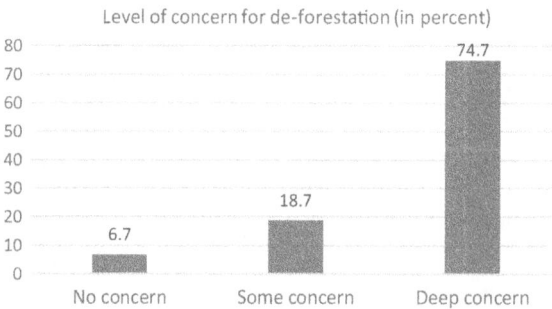

Figure A.16 Concern for deforestation.

Human rights dimension

Do you suffer emotionally or physically
from violence in the family? (in percent)

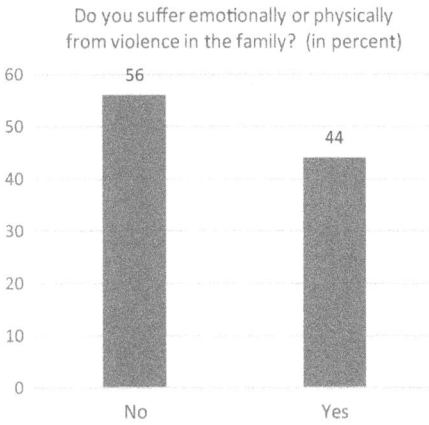

Figure A.17 Family violence affecting emotional/physical health?

Can you talk about political & government
related issues openly & freely?

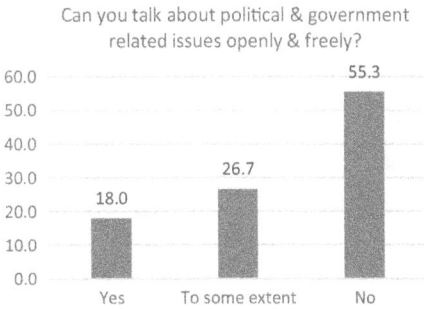

Figure A.18 Able to talk freely about political issues?

To what extent do you have skills/interests
in Women's Political & Social Status? (in
percent)

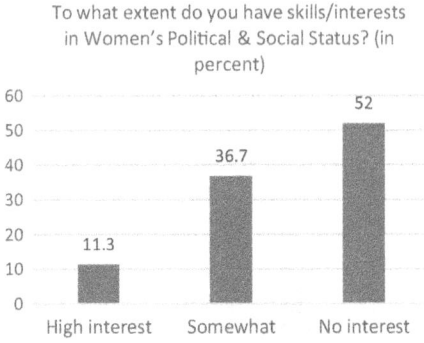

Figure A.19 Skills/interests in women's empowerment socio-political status.

Index